FOOT SOLDIER IN
THE CULTURE WARS

Tony Thomas

Connor Court Publishing

Connor Court Publishing books of essays by Tony Thomas:

That's debatable – 60 years in print (2016)
The West – an insider's tales (2018)
Come to think of it – essays to tickle the brain (2020).

Dedicated to my wonderful, loving wife Marg

Published in 2021 by Connor Court Publishing Pty Ltd

Copyright © Tony Thomas

All rights reserved. No part of this book may be reproduced or transmitted in any form or by any means, electronic or mechanical, including photocopying, recording or by any information storage and retrieval system, without prior permission in writing from the publisher.

Connor Court Publishing Pty Ltd
PO Box 7257
Redland Bay QLD 4165
sales@connorcourt.com
www.connorcourtpublishing.com.au
Phone 0497-900-685

Printed in Australia

ISBN: 9781922449627

Front Cover Image: Briony Thomas

Printed in Australia

Table of Contents

PREFACE — 7

PART ONE:
OVER THE TOP IN THE CLIMATE WARS

Sex Academia-Style: Let's All Have a Tree-some	13
The Curious Avenues of Professorial Inquiry	21
Cool the Planet or We Kill the Dog	28
The Frozen Wastes of the Warmist Mind	34
Feminist Queer Anticolonial Propositions	44
The Asylum Atop Their Ivory Tower	56
The Most Disgusting Climate Cult of All	70
Making Kids Shrill, Scared and Stupid	77
Beware, Parents, Your Kids Are Being 'Scootled'	88
The Australian Academy of Drama Queens	103

PART TWO:
THE BLACK INDUSTRY AT WORK

Who gets to be an "Elder"?	115
The White Privilege of Being Black	120
The Apotheosis of Adam Goodes	135
Another Jaunt up the Garden State Path	149
Bruce Pascoe's Tribe Dines on Young Brains	154
BLM: "Black Landlords Matter"	165

PART THREE:
THEIR ABC'S "IMPARTIALITY"

The ABC's Slip is Showing	171
It's official: ABC Porn for Kids is Fine	181
Some Riots, the Left Kind, Don't Distress the ABC At All	203
Leigh Sales' Most Disgraceful, Biased Interview	216

PART FOUR:
HISTORY & BITS AND PIECES

Freeman Dyson's War by Numbers	227
Battling the Reds in Adelaide	237
Abe Saffron and the Man from ASIO	247
The Hilaria-ous Case of the Pseudo Señora	256
The Academic Murderer: Dr Maurice Benn's Family Tragedy	262
Memories of the Really Wild West	273
The Madman of Tullamarine	282

Preface

This is my 63rd year as a writer – no, I'm not 63, I'm 81 but I began as a cadet journalist on *The West Australian* in 1958. I went to work straight from high school, naïve and opinionated. The West tolerated its cadets' mess-ups and I survived to do a decade's reporting there. I then spent a decade in the Canberra Press Gallery writing economics for *The Age* and 20 years writing business stories with the weekly magazine *BRW*. After retiring in 2001 I wrote essays for fun and to improve the world. I've published close to 400, mostly for Quadrant Online.

Through 2015 I had back aches which I attributed to a tennis strain at my retired-guys' tennis club. In January 2016 my GP announced that multiple myeloma had chewed out my lower vertebrae. I needed backbone reconstruction followed by treatment to stop the myeloma spreading further.

So I thought I'd get a wriggle on and put my essays into a book for posterity. Brisbane's Connor Court published *That's Debatable: 60 years in print*, in 2016.

My Perth journalism scrapbooks somehow followed me around for 60 years and in 2018 I published 75 features I'd penned on life and times in the Sandgroper capital of the 1960s: *The West: An insider's tales*.

My health recovered so I kept writing. In 2020 Connor Court put out my third book, *Come to think of it – essays to tickle the brain*. And now I've gathered much of my recent output into a fourth collection, *Foot soldier in the culture wars*.

Of all my values, free debate is paramount. Next is protecting schoolkids against brainwashing. Primarily, "culture wars" are the Left imposing its ideologies by censorship, "cancelling" people, creating a climate of fear to stifle free debate, and indoctrinating kids. As a lifelong journalist, I could weep to see even mainstream journalists joining the clamour to impose conformity of thought.

Cases in point:

More than 400 news outlets globally, with an alleged reach to 2 billion people, have signed a "climate emergency" pact to ratchet up the future-global-warming scare (truth immaterial) and suppress the contrary views which also happen to be science-based. This group includes seven Australian media outlets and 11 in New Zealand. The Australian Broadcasting Commission, while not a signatory, by policy ignores climate sceptical views. ABC reporters are to maintain "a balance that follows the weight of evidence". The guidelines for staff imply that climate sceptics are akin to anti-vaccination nutters and 9/11 "truthers".

The Left's culture wars have blitzed State education, from pre-school to matriculation. Education Departments are complicit in outsourcing of lessons to green-left groups, particularly *Cool*

Australia which now reaches into 90% of Australian primary and secondary schools. My essay here on the government-sponsored "Scootle" education resources discovers the same bias. Green-leftism is not contrary to official education policy, it's part of it under the "Sustainability" code.

As for universities, surveys show that many students and staff now self-censor rather than provoke the campus Left establishment. The Institute of Public Affairs last year found that only 177 of 1181 courses in literature, history and politics involved our Western intellectual and cultural inheritance. In order, the main courses on offer were Identity Politics (572), "Critical Race Theory" (380) and Gender (306). I've investigated many "gender studies" activities such as a Melbourne University "woke" group worshiping concrete paths and listening respectfully to a NZ expert on tree-humping. (I don't invent stuff, I show that it's really happening).

The wrongful persecution and gaoling of Australia's top Catholic, Cardinal Pell, is typical of culture-war assaults on institutional religion. Earlier, the poorly-named Human Rights Commission hounded three Queensland University of Technology students for non-existent "racism" and made their lives a torment for several years.

The "history wars" continue, with the Left, schools, Melbourne University and the ABC even endorsing the nonsense of professed Aboriginal Bruce Pascoe, who claims pre-contact Aborigines lived in towns, sowed crops and kept livestock (perhaps wombats) in

pens. Woke warriors, with ABC support, also besmirch the pride Australians have in Australia Day by calling it "Invasion Day".

I've enlisted in the culture wars to fight all those barbarians, mainly via ridicule. It helps that "Progressives" are proud and frank about their machinations and idiocies. Authors of abstruse academic papers, for example, imagine that no-one but their groupthink tribe would read them, but in their bilge I often find my diamonds.

For all that, I'm not just a political animal. As Yeats wrote,

> "Too long a sacrifice
> Can make a stone of the heart."

So I love the quirks of suburban life and our arts and our history. When something amuses me, I share it around. A father loves all his children but may I mention my new favourites here? Like *The Curious Avenues of Professorial Inquiry* …

I grew up half-way up the big hill at the east end of Garling Street in Willagee, a Housing Commission cluster fondly dubbed "White Ant City". I was delighted to learn that an academic from Graz via Arizona was studying the emotional traumas of Willagee-ites from climate-caused floods, events resembling Noah's time given that Willagee straddles hills, but strangely I can't recall any floods.

Next, when probing "Feral Feminisms" at highly-rated Sydney University, I was set aback by a portrait of a heavily bearded and tattooed trans-woman called Alok Vaid-Menon:

They will say that femininity is not powerful,' Vaid-Menon acknowledges, 'but i [sic] have stopped traffic simply by going outside'. The stakes of their [sic] *public trans-femininity remain laser clear, still, when they [sic] fantasize, 'what would it mean to no longer have to be fabulous to survive?'*

The ABC has a lame program called "You can't ask that!" about how fat people manage coitus and so on. My own version of "You can't ask that!" is the piece, *Who gets to be an elder?* I'm sure you've wondered who dubbed Aunty Mary with her "Aunty" title, or whether you can be a *younger* elder. Laugh, but for safety these days, laugh only on the inside.

Sandgropers can't shed their birthright and for incredulity, you can't beat my tale of Perth's great manhunt of 1963, when literally thousands of armed citizen-amateurs went gunning for a murderer on the loose in a suburban pine plantation. Check out the details here in *Memories of the Really Wild West*.

Thanks Quadrant Online editor Roger Franklin for your professional handling of my copy. Roger enhances my drafts every time. Finally, praise to my beloved and stoic wife Marg for keeping home fires burning while my head is stuck in the i-clouds.

Enjoy my book. Otherwise, throw it at the cat.

Tony Thomas, 31 May 2021.

PART ONE:
OVER THE TOP IN THE CLIMATE WARS

Sex Academia-Style: Let's All Have a Tree-some

22 April 2020

Picture a climate-conscious Melbourne University arts graduate, Nancy, out of work and applying to stack shelves at Woolies.

> *Recruiter: Any special skills?*
>
> *Nancy: Sure. I did a lot of inter-disciplinary study with the university's flagship Sustainability Society Institute (MSSI).*
>
> *Recruiter: Like what?*
>
> *Nancy: Well, last July 8, I went to an all-day symposium on "Hacking the Anthropocene". MSSI was an overall seed funder and major seminar sponsor, and one of the speakers was an authority on tree humping.*
>
> *Recruiter: I see. What's the "Anthropocene"?*
>
> *Nancy: You really haven't heard of the Climate Emergency and the Anthropocene? It's "a name coined for the emerging geological era in which humans are centralised as the dominant planetary force. Perhaps intended to evoke ecological concern, it draws on*

settler colonial discourse, problematically homogenises all humans as planet destroyers and implies that we are locked into these petrifying ways of being."

Recruiter: We might get back to you. This Wuhan Virus is keeping us pretty busy right now with the empty shelves. Thanks for dropping by.

Nancy's interview was cut short before she could elaborate on that symposium with its "exciting schedule", which featured a keynote talk on "Composting Feminism" (not a misprint).

This Do-It-Together symposium was booked out by eager academics and their students, some fretting on the waitlist. It was at the Abbotsford ex-Convent, with vegan morning tea and lunch and gender-neutral toilets. At least the morning tea wasn't drunk from jam jars, a favored receptacle at MSSI soirees. In each of three sessions, master Anthropocene Hackers described their hacks (example: "Rupturing the colonial Anthropocene"), and the audience got to "hack back", a hip term for discussion. Some participants were "theys" rather than he or she.

The revelations were interleaved with "walkshops" where attendees "weathered with what-ever mid-Winter provides", offset by raincoats and fleecy underwear. Those walkshops were about 'Un-earthing. Wild concrete on living soil', curated by visual ecologist Aviva Reed and celebrating "the sedimentation of our imaginations." Her walk notes are in need of Google Translate, but here goes:

Description: An ethereal moment of material molecular immersion into the living grounds we walk upon. Through this process we will unearth our obligations and responsibilities to care for the soil that cares for us ... This walkshop engages critically and sensually with what is beneath our feet, honouring both the ingredients that make up the concrete pathways that hold us and the soil beneath ... We name and acknowledge the sand, lime, silt and clay and through an immersive process will explore the deep time ... asking what is our responsibility to honour the concrete for both its utilitarian and multi-specied complexity and our obligation to unearth the negations of this concrete for the soil beneath.

Celebrity guest was multi-tattooed and ripped Professor of Gender Studies Jack Halberstam of Columbia University, whose "work considers wild, queer, decolonial possibilities for protest culture, anarchy and performance." Accidentally anticipating the Wuhan Flu, he spoke on "Strategies of Wildness – Why We Must Unbuild the World!"

He was currently working on a book titled *Wild thing: Queer theory after nature* which explores queer anarchy, performance and protest culture as well as the intersections between animality, the human and the environment. His prior books include *Skin Shows: Gothic Horror and the Technology of Monsters, Female Masculinity, The Queer Art of Failure* and *Gaga Feminism: Sex, Gender, and the End of Normal*. His articles include *What's Queer About Queer Studies Now?* Who paid his airfares here, I wonder?

The Composting Feminism speaker was senior gender lecturer Dr Astrida Neimanis, who founded Hacking the Anthropocene in 2016. She hails from (you guessed it) Sydney University. Only last week she was writing about what bushfire smoke and Wuhan Flu "have to teach us about the politics and imaginaries of breathing in contemporary societies? How do 'we' notice, engage with and respond to our gaseous (e.g. oxygen, carbon) and multispecies (e.g. eucalypts, viruses) relations and how might 'we' do this otherwise?" She would like to see you "reflecting on your own experiences of breathing over the last few months, and how this might be similar and different to human and non-human others."

Another talk was by artist Richard Orjis, of the Auckland University of Technology, on 'bttming the Anthropocene'. As for "bttming", there are no safe spaces or trigger warnings here, so think twice before googling it.

Orjis says, "Bttm Methodology emerged out of a drifting conversation about glow worms, mushrooms and queer ecologies, tree hugging/humping, resting, composting and excretion, toilets and cruising."

As an unworldly reporter, I needed to consult Urban Dictionary to discover that actual "tree humping" may involve either sex with or domination of the phallic-like tree, often by exhibitionists. Here's how it is used and defined:

Girl 1: He looks lonely.

Girl 2: Good thing he's tree humping.

Platonic tree-hugging is a fetish practised by many green/climate academics. It was celebrated in a piece by Charles Sturt lecturer Shelby Gull Laird at the monoversity and taxpayer-funded (but anti-free speech) outlet *The Conversation*. "Are we all tree-huggers?" she asked. Her suggestions include "Spend some time sitting under a tree. And if you're so inclined, maybe even give it a cuddle."

The global arts community is not always into trees platonically. Minnesota's Conceptual Artist Genevieve Belleveau, daughter of an environmental educator, has described her psychedelic drug-enhanced tree affairs, starting with a birch tree at age eight:

Fascination, and love, and the sense that the tree accepted my feelings—that even if she didn't love me back, exactly, she was receptive to my love for her ... kissing her and hugging her I felt a kind of shame afterwards, because I did that to a living entity without its consent ... I don't think it's that bad that I humped the tree or whatever.

You're probably thinking my interest in this lady's arboreal love life is just prurient. No, because Ms Belleveau from far off Minnesota picked up on my Quadrant tribute to Melbourne's Ecosexual Bathhouse in 2016, run by Perth's Pony Express with $80,000 tax and ratepayer funding. The Bathhouse, like the symposium backed by Melbourne Sustainable Society Institute, offered a route for surviving the Anthropocene from the "devastating forces unleashed by global capital". Among the Bathhouse's attractive dances were

Slug Sex: The dominatrix uses UV light "to illuminate a trail of goo, which she produces in a graceful, entwining dance. Music is a lugubrious, downbeat, sensual song. Projector displays video of the phenomenal slug copulatory behaviour."

Cuttlefish: The dominatrix slowly approaches audience "and fans them with undersea-like movements, before encircling them in her wings then darting away."

Getting back (with some reluctance) to Auckland's artist Orjis, he explained that "bttming is a methodology for exploring power dynamics, kinship, relationality and passivity as an active resistance to capitalist, colonial and patriarchal reproductive impulses." He earlier ran a Melbourne Sustainable Society Institute workshop on "How can we privilege 'arse end of the world', or southern antipodean orientations? And how might this dismantle dominant epistemologies of the north (rational, Eurocentric, Judeo-Christian)? And how can methods of passive resistance operate in response to colonial, capitalist and patriarchal hegemony?" He advertised that his workshop "will invite participants to engage with these ideas through sitting, thinking, making and talking, or not sitting, not thinking, not making or not talking." That seems to cover the field.

In 2018 Orjis ran an exhibition in Basement Adult Shop & Cruise Club, one of the longest-running owner-operated sex stores and cruise clubs in Aotearoa New Zealand. The show was called, "Under your skin you look divine". He wrote that it "realises the important role sex stores and cruise clubs play in contributing to queer culture and identities" and invited "locally based artists to take over the store in a one-night flirtatious digital queer mess of an exhibition."

Melbourne University's *Hacking the Anthropocene* was not just the Convent seminar but a series of workshops and events over months of "challenging the toxic and corrosive logics of racial and extractive capitalism."

One seminar was to help educators get their message into school classrooms. As convenor Blanche Verlie put it, pre-Wuhan of course:

> *Climate vulnerability-and-complicity, white fragility and supremacy, CIS entitlement and species-ism each present particularly challenging conditions for educators and other pedagogues to navigate in contemporary educational settings.*
>
> *How can we effectively engage people in discussions and responses to what might feel for them – and us – like an existential crisis? As educators, communicators, artists, activists, scholars, facilitators, parents, children or others, what are the strategies we are using to engage people with issues such as (but not limited to) climate change, the ongoing colonisation of Indigenous peoples, xenophobia or homophobia, or mass extinction? What are the specific characteristics of how such issues play out in classrooms (or other spaces)?*

The welfare, sanity and usefulness to society of the student

generation is obviously in safe hands with Melbourne University academics and their colleagues. No matter who else in the Australian workforce is losing their jobs, the government must support as providers of "essential services" the academics engaged in Anthropocene Hacks, Feminist Composting and tree humping.
#

PART 1

The Curious Avenues of Professorial Inquiry

12 May 2020

Professor Petra Tschakert at the University of Western Australia is halfway through a project to "locate loss from climate change in everyday places". These places include my very own Perth stamping ground of Willagee.

Heavens, my parents moved to Willagee in late 1953, when it was raw sand. Willagee featured the Housing Commission's half-finished jerry-built houses, for wharf toilers like my stepfather and low-lifes like our neighbours. I say jerry-built because, for example, our bath was cracked. The Commission installed a replacement, also cracked. We lived with it. My parents died but my big sister to this day is a Willagee girl. No-one knows more about 67 years of climate change impacts in Willagee, if any, than my sister and I.

I write all this with trepidation. I was backlashed when I last wrote about Willagee in 1981. Bob Gottliebsen had just started *Business Review Weekly* and for a year I had to write all the Letters to the Editor. It was boring, and as a family in-joke I wrote myself a letter urging capital gains tax on family homes, and signed it, "G. Princip, Willagee, WA". Someone from Perth wrote us a real and blistering response saying there was no G. Princip of Willagee on the electoral roll. The rotter had noticed my G. Princip might be the same Gavrilo Princip who shot the Archduke and started the First World War. After reflecting for several seconds, we threw that complaint in the bin.

Anyway, Geography Professor Tschakert is discovering — with the help of a $353,000 research grant from grateful taxpayers — how my sister and I, plus other Willagee types, manage our climate "grief and hope". Innovatively, she helps us cope with our "intolerable losses".

Her four-year study also covers suburban Attadale and Kelmscott, further-out Darlington, and the wheatbelt towns of Toodyay, Northam, Merredin and Southern Cross. The research is not just academic folderol. She claims two significant benefits: "from this science of loss" she will do a "critical analysis" of our "community resilience in the face of socio-economic and environmental threats". She will also sool town planners from the government to help us. Her broad aim is to see how the ghastly impacts of climate change, namely "fire, drought and flooding", are putting our deepest values at risk.

Memo to Dr Tschakert: It would take a Noah's Ark extreme event to flood Willagee. It's on several big hills.

Fires? The only Willagee fire I can remember is when some lousy brats lit our Guy Fawkes' bonfire the day before and ran off laughing. Drought? Our lawn sprinklers doused the grass all morning in the Fifties and Sixties. For dam shortages since, blame The Greens.

The professor's project also embraces Willagee's near-neighbour, Attadale, a riverside joint once home to Heath Ledger and cricketers Mitchell and Shaun Marsh. Not much flood, fire and drought there either.

Her third suburb, Kelmscott, did suffer a bushfire in 2011, lit by some idiot on his private block in defiance of a windy fire-ban day. There'd been drought-fuelled build-up of grass and dry bush — nothing whatsoever to do with global warming. Ex-Resources Minister Matt Canavan last March forced sheepish CSIRO top brass to admit they had no studies demonstrating a link between climate change, fire weather and bushfires. Likewise, top climate crusader Dr Andy Pitman, of UNSW, publicly let slip last June there was no reason why global warming should worsen droughts, rather the contrary. Since both Pitman and Tschakert are IPCC top lead authors it's time they got their stories aligned.

I don't really understand Willagee's climate grief because the latest HadCrut global temp trend shows a mere 0.8degC warming trend in the past 80 years. For most Willagee veterans, the priority is flogging their blocks to developers in a dud real estate market.

As for the professor's concern for safeguarding our values, my Willagee family knows a lot about values. We got kicked out of our rented home on Stirling-highway, Nedlands in 1953 and wound up in "Mulberry Farm", a decrepit ex-air force camp near Fremantle. Mum has written of it as

> this pinched little settlement where the homeless and dispossessed of the city were herded ... Nights erupted into fights, the crash of breaking bottles, torrents of abuse between couples run ragged by the tension of waiting [for a Commission home], dogs barking in sympathy, an altercation that took a serious turn, a burly axe-wielder chasing a woman shouting, 'Don't you try that trick again, you bitch!' followed by the shriek of a police car siren.

Stepfather Vic lumped sacks "down hold", the wharf's most dangerous and dirty work:

> Bags of asbestos sometimes broke in the sling hanging from the high crane and showered men with the stuff. Only later did they know it to be deadly, even to women washing their overalls.

Bad as the job was, it was worse when Vic caught the bus to "Freo" (Fremantle) and got no job at the morning pickup, wasting his morning and his fares.

Finally came the letter offering us a cottage in Willagee (nicknamed "White-Ant City"). We lived a week inside by candlelight until the electricity came on from Collie fossil fuel, but we didn't mind those CO_2 emissions.

Our neighbours comprised a man prone to beating his slatternly wife. Their feral kids and dogs all had fleas. The wife would lament to us that her oldest was "a ba-a-a-d boy!" hinting at misdeeds involving his sister and even herself. The least of his bad habits was throwing fire-crackers into the dunny, causing his mother to scream as she sat.

Mum at some point in exasperation told the husband to "drop dead". Two days later he and I were walking to the bus stop and a snappy mongrel jumped at him. He slid to the ground dead of a heart attack or stroke. Mum went in to console the widow. "'e was the breadwinner," she sobbed.

Their youngest boy grew up to serve a long stretch for rape. Mum provided the judge a character reference based on his hopelessly compromised Willagee upbringing.

Opposite our house was a newly-planted pine plantation on land owned by the incredibly wealthy University of Western Australia. We watched it grow for 40 years. It was cut down for suburban plots about the same year my folks paid off their mortgage.

Willagee today is gentrifying fast, swanky bungalows replacing the fibro-clad Commission homes. But pockets of old Willagee remain, including a dusky cohort that led to the Archibald Street liquor outlet becoming a steel-clad fortress against break-ins.

Dr Tschakert can use any of this in her peer-reviewed report, free of charge. I fancy it's as good as her own output.

For example, she thinks recent bushfires, floods and cyclones are uniquely extreme. They ain't. Not a climate modeller herself, she expresses touching faith in the mainstream IPCC models, of which 111 of 114 runs exaggerated the warming trends, according to the IPCC itself. She thinks it "reckless" to ignore the models' forecasts and worst-case scenarios, which the IPCC in 2001 said must by definition be bogus. She needs to read the devastating critiques of climate forecasting models by oceanic modeller Dr Mototaka Nakamura (MIT, Duke, Jet Propulsion Laboratory):

> *These models completely lack some critically important climate processes and feedbacks, and represent some other critically important climate processes and feedbacks in grossly distorted manners to the extent that makes these models totally useless for any meaningful climate prediction.*

Professor Tschakert specialises in people's "anticipatory" grief over global warming, i.e., stuff that hasn't happened yet and might never happen: *"There is fantastic research that shows how to embrace grief and loss in an anticipatory way. A term that is used is anticipatory history."*

She also appears to disparage individual resilience to climate because the nanny state ought to fix things:

> *... the Australian states would like to see their citizens ideally as resilient citizens that can adapt by themselves, that can make the right choices but on their own, (they) ought to be reinventing themselves to take care of something which, really, truthfully, ought to be the responsibility of the state.*

Dr Tschakert seems unduly lugubrious, writing papers like "One thousand ways to experience loss: A systematic analysis of climate-related intangible harm from around the world." She needs to look up tangibles like global agricultural yields. After a half-century of warming and extra CO_2, yields for wheat, barley, rice, soybeans, spuds, and bananas continue to rise. On just about any indicator of health and well-being, the globe's population has never been better off (ChiCom virus and ChiCom threats excepted).

In another co-authored paper called "A science of loss" she also plumbs "strategies for embracing and managing grief". A co-author was Melbourne Uni's Jon Barnett who had enough common sense to call b/s on Extinction Rebellion zealots at Melbourne University last December, much to their indignation. I clearly recognise Barnett's hand in this minatory paragraph:

> *Predictions of loss may themselves contribute to loss. Dramatic narratives about future crises have been shown to influence the risk of crises occurring. Several studies explain how talk of catastrophic climate futures rarely leads to mitigation and adaptation but instead results in fatalism, self-blame, underinvestment in vulnerable places, and even accelerated degradation of natural resources.*

I did some "anticipatory history" of my own by attending Tschakert's lecture at Sydney University next August titled "Epistemic Violence and Slow Emergencies in Today's Climate Justice: A Provocation". The problems of time travel compounded when the lecture was virus-postponed indefinitely but I still caught the gist of it, Captain Kirk-style. She asked,

> *How do we find our ways within these emerging dilemmas [re basic climate justice] without losing track of core development goals in the Anthropocene and our commitment to decolonizing development and disaster scholarship?*

It does all really make sense, or would if there actually was any "Anthropocene".

The $64 question is how much Willagee temperatures have actually risen in the past century or so. The answer is 1degC, or nearly that. I can't see how this small increase over 100 years can cause anyone much inconsolable grief and loss. I wouldn't notice 1decC change over five minutes, let alone 70 years.

In any case my sister and I can now buy ample Kleenex at Willagee's Archibald Street IGA to mop our climate tears. #

Cool the Planet or We Kill the Dog

12 May 2021

My spaniel, Natasha, has outworn her welcome at our house. According to apex climate scientists doing their peer-reviewed work at universities, dogs and cats are harming the planet with their substantial carbon footprints (make that pawprints). I should replace Natasha, they say, with more climate-friendly pets like galahs, edible hens and rabbits, hamsters, and tortoises. If anyone's got cause for climate grief, it's Natasha.

They calculate that Natasha's emissions stem largely from growing the meat in her pet food. There's also the plastic poop bags that I sneak into other people's red bins during her walks. Her CO2 emissions are about 30kg a year. That's not counting her direct emissions while we're trying to watch Kate Winslet slumming it in *Mare of Easttown*.

The tipping point to ditch the bitch and cull the kitten could be as early as 2023, a mere two years hence. That's according to Harvard Professor Naomi Oreskes, a doyenne of the catastrophist community. No-one can doubt her credentials. Wiki lists her latest award as the Medal of the British Academy (2019) amid 27 climate honors, such as "Ambassador and Fellow, American Geophysical Union" and "Francis Bacon Award in the History and Philosophy of Science and Technology, Caltech".

In 2010 she wrote the solemn book *Merchants of Doubt: How a Handful of Scientists Obscured the Truth on Issues from Tobacco Smoke to Global*

Warming. She's followed up with an even scarier tract, *The Collapse of Western Civilisation*. In this book she says global warming will "wipe out" every Australian man, woman and child. Only a few scattered communities — some mountain people in South America, for instance — will survive the killer heating.

More importantly, she prophesises the agonising climate deaths of those puppies and kittens. One reader, she says,

> *started crying when the pets die, so I didn't mean to upset people too much ... I was just trying to come up with something that I thought people wouldn't forget about, and I thought, well, Americans spend billions of dollars every year taking care of their pets, and I thought if people's dogs started dying, maybe then they would sit up and take notice.*

I looked up that bit in her book, and found the Kitten and Puppy Mass Extinction occurs in 2023, along with the climate deaths of 500,000 people and $US500 billion financial damage. Oreskes writes, in bold type no less:

> *The loss of pet cats and dogs garnered particular attention among wealthy Westerners, but what was anomalous in 2023 soon became the new normal. A shadow of ignorance and denial had fallen over people who considered themselves children of the Enlightenment.*

She was interviewed by the ABC's science guru Robyn Williams AO AM, a Fellow of the Australian Academy of Science and also showered with awards and three honorary doctorates.[1] He enthused with

---

1   His partner, Jonica Newby, is both an ABC veteran and a veteran veterinarian. Last March she published *Beyond Climate Grief*. It's about "How do we find cour-

her:

> *Yes, not only because it's an animal but it's local. You see, one criticism of the scientists is they're always talking about global things ... And so if you are looking at your village, your animals, your fields, your park, your kids, and the scientists are talking about a small world that you know, then it makes a greater impact, doesn't it.*

Oreskes responded:

> *Well, exactly. It was about bringing it literally home, literally into your home, your family, your pet, the dog or cat that you love who is your faithful and trusted companion.*

But surely Oreskes' pet doom forecast isn't (trademarked) Peer-Reviewed Science? Yes, her book is kosher, she verifies.

> *Well, it's all based on solid science. Everything in this book is based on the scientific projections from the Intergovernmental Panel on Climate Change. All we did was to add to the social and human aspects to it.*

Back in the real world, the ABC introduced the Oreskes episode on its Science Show with a typical lie: "The Earth's climate is changing at the highest of predicted rates." Fact: The past 40 years' warming to date is barely half of what the orthodox modelling predicted.[2]

---

age when climate change overwhelms us emotionally?"

[2] I forced the ABC to add the following to its iview page: *Editor's note: The original introduction stated that "Earth's climate is changing at the highest of predicted rates, scientists have given up on the much talked about two degree ceiling." In context these words telegraphed the premise on which Prof Oreskes' work of fiction is based; however, it has been interpreted as a statement of incontrovertible fact and has therefore been removed to prevent any further misunderstanding.*

This ABC wallow was all a while back, but there's now a veritable industry of scholarship damning our pets' CO2 emissions. Tax-funded full-time climate scientists have assessed the climate impact of St Bernards vs Labradors vs Jack Russells. But two studies on dogs' climate footprints are at loggerheads – one from Australian researchers, the other from Arizona. As a patriot, I support the Australian results showing the CO2 emissions as St Bernard, 90kg; Labrador, 60kg and Jack Russell 20kg. The Arizonans plumped for 20-30 times higher emissions: this is not yet settled science.

The assault on our four-legged friends hit Code Red last month, with Vox magazine USA headlining, "Are our pets gobbling up the planet?" It's sub-headed, ominously: "Pet care is unarguably bad for the environment. What can we do about it?"

The piece, copiously illustrated, noted that during COVID lockdowns lots of households acquired new pets, aggravating the global heating emergency. It quoted Gregory Okin, a geography professor at the University of California, Los Angeles: "Reducing the rate of dog and cat ownership, perhaps in favour of other pets that offer similar health and emotional benefits, would considerably reduce these impacts."

One learned estimate is that a medium dog needs 0.84 hectares of arable land for its pet food. That's more than the ecological footprint of a Fourth World citizen, and twice the ecological footprint of a 4.6 litre LandCruiser doing 10,000km a year. Even a cat's ecological pawprint equals that of a VW Golf, or so said a pair of British academic pet specialists, lately educating New Zealanders from

Victoria University, Wellington.[3]

Professors Robert and Brenda Vale wrote a book, *Time to Eat the Dog?* Responding to a public outcry, Robert said, "We need to know what we're doing when it comes to the environment. We can't go blind into this debate. Nothing should be off limits no matter how uncomfortable it is to discuss it."

Their book title was deliberately provocative: don't expect breast of kelpie from Coles. They didn't want pups and kittens culled, let alone eaten, but they'd have no problem with tinned rats for cats, or dog-owners switching to pet rabbits and boiling the bunnies' offspring for lunch.

The smaller the pet, they say, the better for the planet. It was Woody Allen who claimed his parents gave him an ant for a pet, which or whom he called "Spot". If bikie gangs had any climate conscience, they'd use chihuahuas and Pomeranians to guard their clubhouses instead of mastiffs and Rhodesian Ridgebacks.

A 2019 study reported that the average Dutch dog's carbon emissions just for food were up to 1.4 tonnes and cats were up to 0.25 tonnes. (Cats win again). This is nearly double the annual electricity carbon emissions for the average UK household just for dog food and about a third of household electricity emissions for cat's food.

The 160-odd million pets in the US create 64 million tonnes of greenhouse emissions, equal to 13 million cars, says one of those sci-

---

[3] Robert Vale's retired, his wife Brenda is a Professorial Research Fellow.

encey papers in PLOS ONE, which boasts "rigorous peer review".

Moreover, humans and their pets are getting obese at similar rates. People replicate their food fads with pet foods, with about a year's lag. Thus we get "No Carb" and Paleo Diet pet foods. Fido's tin of lamb hotpot may now include rice, pearly barley, broccoli, spinach, blueberries, flaxseed, marigold petals, burdock root and alfalfa. That certainly sounds better on a label than cheaper pet food's "hydrolysed feathers", horse, Skippy and "animal derivatives" like hair, teeth and bowels.

Some climate scientists have flogged the reverse narrative that pets are victims rather than culprits of the global heating emergency. They scare the punters with tales that warming will worsen pets' ticks, fleas and heartworms.

The climate scientists now want legal limits on the type and number of our pets. Although I am older than 17 and not as learned as Greta Thunberg, I still intend to mobilise schoolchildren the world over (except China) for a School Strike for Labradoodles. We march on Federal Parliament next week with our Staffies, groodles, spoodles and cavoodles, and your Siamese, Persians, Abyssinians, Maine Coons and Ragdolls. Cavalier King Charleses, united, will never be defeated. (Cavalier King Charles 1, admittedly, lost his head).

Further Reading: *7 signs you love your pet more than your partner.*[4] For example: You return from grocery shopping with a basket of treats for your dog and forget the one thing your partner asked for. #

---

4   www.homestolove.com.au

The Frozen Wastes of the Warmist Mind

16 February 2021

On New Year's Eve I took a $3000 seat on an overnight 787 Dreamliner from Tullamarine down to the Antarctic and back. It was sensational to see some of this mysterious, beautiful and inhospitable continent by the light of the midnight sun, in crystal-clear air and from a low altitude. Not so pleasant was the tour-guide commentary from a couple of old hands from the Australian base, one a glaciologist and the other once an Antarctic maintenance plumber. The cockpit crew weighed in too with descriptions and opinions.

The pair of 70,000lb-thrust engines provided a low whining accompaniment to the talks. But there was already plenty of verbal whining, as if each talker wanted to outdo the others on the perils of global warming in the Antarctic. I cocked an ear briefly but then tuned out, as every speaker was talking nonsense. Normally, I'd have taken down their verbiage in shorthand to pillory them in print. But I was rivetted by the views as glaciers came and went, sea ice dotted the coastline and the smoking crater of Mt Erebus hove into sight. So I'll just summarise: they blamed global warming for everything down there that moved, and everything there that didn't move as well.

I think they had guilty consciences. After all, we were polluting the pristine Antarctic air with jet-A1 exhaust gases, and our plane was full of elitists (myself included). We cheerfully paid as much as $7000 for a night's trip to regions off-limits to 99.9 per cent of Australians. Sure, the Antarctica flights business professes to be carbon neutral by donating to things like the Yarra Yarra Biodiversity Project, near Geraldton in Western Australia. If we really believed in fairy tales about the looming Year 2100 hothouse extinction, we'd be building dykes in Port Melbourne and lunching on lentils.

Our commentators were either out of touch or fibbing: the Antarctic is not warming. Sea ice there is growing, not contracting. The Antarctic refutes the climate modelling orthodoxy that global warming will be amplified at the poles relative to the equator.

Here's a paper that appeared in Nature just last October: "Low Antarctic continental climate sensitivity due to high ice sheet orography [mountains]". It's by Hansi A. Singh & Lorenzo M. Polvani:

> *The Antarctic continent has not warmed in the last seven decades, despite a monotonic [steady] increase in the atmospheric concentration of greenhouse gases ... Antarctic sea ice area has modestly expanded and warming has been nearly non-existent over much of the Antarctic ice sheet.*

The paper uses modelling to blame the non-warming on the high altitude of the Antarctic land mass. Nice try — except real modelling experts says these "state of the art" models are incapable of dealing with climate complexities, being especially ignorant about clouds, thunderstorms and future solar irradiance. Meanwhile, scientists by the dozen have been scrabbling for explanations about why their pet hypothesis is a dud in the Antarctic, e.g., the ozone hole and even a "negative greenhouse effect".

There appears to have been a bit of warming along Antarctica's Western Peninsula, which scientists of warmist bent bang on about interminably. However, in 2017 researchers discovered no fewer than 91 subsurface volcanos well matching the geographic peninsula hotspots. Some were as big as the 4000-metre Mount Eiger. This Antarctic science is not exactly "settled". Meanwhile, a lot of scientific commentary simply invents a warming narrative down there to bolster their "climate emergency" nonsense.

There are 19 temperature stations in the Antarctic with long track records. It would seem useful to analyse the readouts. Maybe, unlike applying for research grants, that's too sophisticated a task for "climate scientists". Luckily there is young lay blogger in Japan who calls herself "Kirye" and has downloaded and graphed the 30-years of data from NASA records. She finds around half of the 19 stations show no warming or slight cooling, and the minor warming of the others is "nothing unusual". Two stations show slight warming but are near the South Pole, where the mean temperature is 50 degrees below freezing, so their fractional warming is hardly enough to melt any ice sheets.

Kirye did a further check of 13 temperature stations along the West Peninsular (about which all sorts of horror-show predictions are constantly bruited), plus some stations on Antarctic islands to the north. She found all 13 showed slight cooling over the past 20 years. Let me pause here for a personal aside about the incoherent rage that mere mention Antarctic cooling can incite. At a charity club's social gathering in January, I was told to shut up because "no-one is interested in your sceptic crap".

Professor Chris Turney, like my uncharitable social nemesis, was convinced the Antarctic has been warming, and eight years ago he and his Pied Piper followers got badly stuck in the ice on the Good Ship Climate Change aka the *Akademik Shokalskiy* aka Ship of Fools. Much the same happened to climate warriors who imagined they could take their rowboat happily into and through the "melting Arctic".

As for the land-based Greenland ice sheet, it's been growing for the past five years, along with some major Greenland glaciers. Have you heard about Glacier Girl, the P38 twin-boom fighter that force-landed on the Greenland ice in 1942? Ice has increased and the plane 50 years later was found 82 metres below the surface.

In 1903 Roald Amundsen's small boat traversed the North-West Passage, and a small ship made it in 1942. Further back, Vikings settled in Greenland around 1000AD because it offered relatively warm green pastures.

After my Antarctic jaunt I flipped through climate books at Readings Carlton, where there are scores in stock, and observed how authors really let their heads go about the Antarctic. Know-all Barry Jones writes in *What Is To Be Done?* ($29.99, and described as "essential reading"): "If large areas of the Antarctic ice sheet and Greenland were to melt, it would lead to significant sea-level rise and risk drowning major urban coastal cities and towns." That's a big 'if', Baz.

Gillen D'Arcy Wood, professor of "environmental humanities and English" at the University of Illinois and originally from Australia, writes in *Land of Wondrous Cold* ($31.56) that losses from Antarctic melting will top a trillion dollars annually by 2050, plus lead to 200 million climate refugees worldwide. The UN Environment Program (UNEP) in 2005 forecast 50 million climate refugees by 2010. When they failed to show up, UNEP furtively advanced the date to 2020. Hey, UNEP, where are they all? It's 2021! Wood continues that after 2100, things will get worse: stand by for over 200 feet of sea-level rise. Humankind will be like the Patagonians, he ventilates, leading brutish lives before dying out on their unrecognisable shrunken continents.

The fabulist animal fancier David Attenborough, in *A life On Our Planet*, (Kindle $15.99) frets about a billion people in 2100 fleeing 500 coastal cities, like Miami, and another billion farmers trekking to cooler climes. "In the background the sixth mass extinction would become unstoppable," he writes. If you're prone to depression, don't even think of buying Attenborough's book.

For some reason feminists adore the Antarctic. In late 2019, 112 ladies, each with at least a Bachelor degree, went down there on the *Hebridean Sky*, touring 10 bases in three weeks and doubtless distracting the real scientists from their work. The Antarctic Peninsula is one of the fastest-warming places on the planet, they claimed ignorantly. Their expedition, at $A40,000 a head, was subsidised by a Spanish renewables pork-trougher Accione, "to promote women in science diplomacy and climate action." These massed female expeditions were an annual event for the prior three years and, of course, all were claimed to be carbon neutral.

The expeditions are the brainchild of Melbourne-based women's leadership consultant Fabian Dattner and her "Homeward Bound" program. She aims to send a total 1000 women down with the support of woke UN hypocrites like Christiana "Tinkerbell" Figueres.

The women had supranormal powers, apparently, as they claimed to have observed "with our naked eyes" the melting of the glaciers, the oceans warming and, "with breaking hearts", the dying of the wildlife. As at play-school, they decorated the ship's walls with their cheerful drawings. The women took inspiration from *Sur*, a novel which imagines a group of nine South American women beating Raold Amundsen to the South Pole in 1909-10. The plot is used

> *to ironically criticize and then undo both misogyny and colonialism. The nine women of Sur destroy the entire masculinity of explorations when they secretly arrive at the Pole before the official discovery by Amundsen and refuse to leave behind a mark of their success. The narrator recalls she was glad 'for some man longing to be first might come some day, and find it, and know then what a fool he had been, and break his heart.'*

In somewhat circular reasoning, the 112 women tourists, having joined about 55,000 other visitors that year, "agonised" about the harms tourists like themselves do to Antarctica. Conversations were lugubrious as they "discussed the despair and depression about climate change". One woman ecologist said she'd already felt "full-blown panic" over the "dying" Barrier Reef (she needs counselling by sacked Professor Peter Ridd), and she began "prepping" supplies in case of societal breakdown. "It felt like it's all going to unravel, like what's going to be next, the forests?" she said. "Everything is dying so fast, things are disappearing before we can even understand them." I hope she included a shotgun to drive other families from her dugout.

They lamented that their children were "suffering from climate anxiety" and from worry about the planet's future. Maybe they ought to let kids enjoy their childhood, rather than subject them to terror.

Fabian Dattner explains, "We are not custodians and stewards, we are conquerors and rapacious consumers. And so, we are now officially an outbreak species."

The Homeward Bound ladies are relatively sensible compared with those engaged in the new field of feminist glacier research. A key paper, funded from a $US413,000 grant from the US government's National Science Foundation, was the work of a team led by Professor Mark Carey at the University of Oregon — the professor writing through a 'feminist lens'. The other male, Alessandro Antonello, is an environmental history post-grad, who acquired his credentials at the University of Canberra.

The paper — I'm not kidding — is titled "Glaciers, gender, and science: A feminist glaciology framework for global environmental change research." The epic, 15,000-word monograph cites Sheryl St Germain's rightfully obscure 2001 novel, *To Drink a Glacier*, where the author is in the throes of her midlife sexual awakening. She

> interprets her experiences with Alaska's Mendenhall Glacier as sexual and intimate. When she drinks the glacier's water, she reflects:

> That drink is like a kiss, a kiss that takes in the entire body of the other ... like some wondrous omnipotent liquid tongue, touching our own tongues all over, the roofs and sides of our mouths, then moving in us and through to where it knows ... I swallow, trying to make the spiritual, sexual sweetness of it last.

Continuing in the tradition of '50 Shades of Ice', the paper further cites Uzma Aslam Khan's (2010) short story 'Ice, Mating'. The story

> explores religious, nationalistic, and colonial themes in Pakistan, while also featuring intense sexual symbolism of glaciers acting upon a landscape. Khan writes: *'It was Farhana who told me that Pakistan has more glaciers than anywhere outside the poles. And I've seen them! I've even seen them* **fuck!***'* (emphasis in original)

Icy conditions normally inhibit tumescence, but the paper's four authors seem to be in a state of sustained arousal. To them, even ice core drilling evokes coital imagery:

> *Structures of power and domination also stimulated the first large-scale ice core drilling projects – these archetypal masculinist*

> *projects to literally penetrate glaciers and extract for measurement and exploitation the ice in Greenland and Antarctica.*

In passing, and just to tick another of the progressive boxes, the study notes that climate change "can lead to the breakdown of stereotypical gender roles and even gender renegotiation", whatever that may be. (Godden, 2013).

The Australian Homeward Bound circus gets a mention in the paper, to do with a program for smashing 'stereotypical and masculinist practices of glaciology.' The program sent 78 international women to Antarctica in late 2016 to 'explore how women at the leadership table might give us a more sustainable future', the paper says.

By about 7000 words into Carey's paper, readers are subsumed in an Alice in Wonderland discourse. The Cold War, we learn, was apparently not about the contest with the Communist bloc, but a tussle "pursued by a particular group of men as policy-makers who were products of specific elite masculinities (Dean, 2003), operating in the context of anxieties about American masculinities (Cuordileone, 2005), and with particular discourses of masculinity and male bodies, especially in distant places like the Arctic (Farish, 2010.)"

The study includes citation of Scottish visual artist Katie Paterson, who made long-playing records out of glacier melt-water. These LPs play glacier whines and other noises for ten minutes until the ice disks themselves melt. Maybe caution is needed with 240-volt apparatus.

PART 1

The paper insists on respect for folk knowledge about glaciers. Yukon indigenous women, for example, say glaciers are easily excited by bad people who cook nearby with smelly grease, but glaciers can be placated by the quick-witted, the good and the deferential. Cooked food, especially fat, "might grow into a glacier overnight if improperly handled". Such narratives

> *demonstrate the capacity of folk glaciologies to diversify the field of glaciology and subvert the hegemony of natural sciences ... the goal is to understand that environmental knowledge is always based in systems of power discrepancies and unequal social relations, and overcoming these disparities requires accepting that multiple knowledges exist and are valid within their own contexts.*

Here is the study's ringing conclusion:

> *Merging feminist postcolonial science studies and feminist political ecology, the feminist glaciology framework generates robust analysis of gender, power, and epistemologies in dynamic social-ecological systems, thereby leading to more just and equitable science and human-ice interactions.*

It's evening tipple time: could someone please add ice to my Barossa Pearl? #

Feminist Queer Anticolonial Propositions

10 June 2020

Sydney University's vice-chancellor, Michael Spence, is badgering the federal government for research funding to replace the fee losses from what was its pre-COVID 39 per cent international enrolment. I'm sure his university's medical and scientific research is valuable but I don't know about the campus's feminism/gender research output. I also notice that nine of Spence's professors and another five faculty types pledged allegiance to Extinction Rebellion last September, and wonder why they expect continued state funding to subvert civic laws and institutions?

I agree with Spence that, as he looks for $270 million worth of economies, no area should be sacrosanct (except his pace-setting $1.5m remuneration package).

However, my focus on Sydney University research in this article involves its program since 2016, "Hacking the Anthropocene". I'll also review the Canada-based peer-reviewed journal *Feral Feminisms* promoted by the university, with its Sydney Environment Institute calling for submissions last month. Sydney and Melbourne university guest editors will Hack the Anthropocene and also the Capitalocene, Plantatitionocene (sic) and the Cthulucene (sic, should be Cthulhucene, not that it matters. Cthulhucene: an ongoing temporality that resists figuration and dating and demands myriad names).

The previous Issue 9.2 featured poet Alok Vaid-Menon, who

extols his or "their" beauty in a video clip.

> 'They will say that femininity is not powerful,' Vaid-Menon acknowledges, 'but i [sic] have stopped traffic simply by going outside'. The stakes of their public transfemininity remain laser clear, still, when they fantasize, 'what would it mean to no longer have to be fabulous to survive?'

I'll return to *Feral Feminisms* later but will first deal with the university's Hacking the Anthropocene (etc) seminars.

This venture began in April 2016 as "Feminist Queer Anticolonial Propositions" under the auspices of its foundation Sydney Environment Institute. The opening "family-friendly" SEI event featured "a unique gastronomic experience". The invitation says,

> *Participants at this evening of art, conversation, exploration, and digestion will be encouraged to show their debt to (un)charismatic others and ask the world of invisible beings about what our common futures might hold.*

Interdisciplinary US artist, the aptly-named Kathy High, set the tone with a "multimedia and interactive exploration of the power of poo. It investigates our intimate relation to the gut microbiome and asks whose poo would make you a superstar." Usefully, a following discussion "Volatising Bouquet" involved smell research. As speaker Stephanie Springgay, a Toronto associate professor (why do the names sound so meaningful?) put it,

> *When smells are taken into the body for survival or pleasure, we open up our body to that which is not us; to the other ...*

The nose and climate-empowering evening was rounded off with a talk "Caution, workers below", by environmental artist Perdita Phillips, "exploring the boundaries between human and nonhuman worlds". Her accessory was "a modified ouija board, designed to communicate with the world of termites."

The symposium series founder was Sydney University gender lecturer Dr. Astrida Neimanis, "co-hosted in 2017/2018 by Dr. Jennifer Hamilton of Composting [no misprint] Feminisms at Sydney University." The symposium has had three annual runs in Sydney, culminating in 2018 with sessions at the Sydney University Womens' College on "What do we want?" The answer turned out to be "excellent coffee and snacks". Neimanis and Hamilton blurbed,

> *From the desirous pull of the fossil fuelled high-life to grass roots activist demands ('what do we want?'), we ask if it is possible to pursue both extravagant pleasure and intersectional, intergenerational justice. We hope you can join us for a day of communal thought, wild performance and excellent coffee and snacks (you know you want it).*

Last year the scholarly research-fest migrated to Melbourne. There it featured an imported NZ scholarly expert on tree-humping and "walkshop" people honouring the ingredients of concrete in pathways (seriously).

But let's get back to the 2016 inaugural symposium. I'm upset to have missed the "Howling the Anthropocene!" talk by Wollongong University's Genders Professor Fiona Probyn-Rapsey (now with

Sydney Uni and exploring, among other things, "critical whiteness studies").

She was described "a leading scholar in the field of Animal Studies, which she approaches from a feminist postcolonial perspective." She explains the anthropocenic howling like this:

> *Consider the dingo howl — not wild but periurban. How does a dingo, once tethered to a sanctuary fence, her body bearing old wounds of cigarette burns, learn to howl alongside the howling of inmates? The howling of inmates together, started off by one, joined by others – is a sound for the anthropocene — a goodnight, a nightmare, a prisoners [sic] lament, a warning, an eery [sic] embrace, a speculation, an agreement to sing along, a wave at the outside.*

Another speaker, possibly taking the urine on the whole show, was Regrette Etcetera, talking on "Stretch Marx: Oestrogenic Ecosystems, Solastalgia, and Species-Panic in the Capitalocene". She self-touted as "a Sydney-based DJ, performer, artist, activist, whore etcetera, with a set of marketable identity descriptors that land university gigs like this."

Ms Etcetera's talk was

> *a chirpily chiliastic whirlwind tour of some ambivalent Anthropocenes, tracing productive pollutions in Natures flooded with 'gender- bending xenoestrogens', and following the species-panics of an imperilled whiteness through the great 'shemale-ing of humanity' and on into an unknown land beyond Capitalism.*

The next 2017 "Hacking" by the cutting-edge Sydney Uni research crowd was about "weathering". It was supported by the Sydney

Environment Institute, the Sydney Social Sciences and Humanities Advanced Research Centre, a Swedish arts bunch and the ARC Centre of Excellence for the History of Emotions.

One speaker was fashionista Lisa Heinze on "What to Wear to Weather the End of the World as We Know It: A Future Fashion Manifesto." I had suspected she was also taking the urine, but she turned out to be a sustainable lifestyle advocate currently pursuing a PhD on sustainable fashion at the University of Sydney … and "a Fashion Revolution committee member" tackling fashion "for an environmentally and socially just future."

Drs Neimanis and Hamilton were doubly pained about the Anthropocene because of its racial whiteness.

> *Moving 'Towards the idea of a black Anthropocene' would re-centre that which is already centred in the Anthropocene—race—and would move against the implicit structural whiteness of the Anthropocene … potentially towards other more accountable, decolonised, geosocial futures.*

The Anthropocene was also danced by arts specialists for the 2019 Sydney Festival, after a week-long workshop led by five choreographers, once more with Sydney Environment Institute en pointe. As sponsors explain,

> *The point is not to paint, or write, or dance, the scalar immensity of the Anthroprocene into a single paragraph or snapshot. This would just reinforce the Anthropocene's seeming distance from our lived experience. Instead, arts and humanities endeavours find ways to make connections to that more-than-human scale through*

the sensory apparatuses of our bodies: a tastebud finds a pathway to a history of colonialism; the affective tenor of a metaphor brings us into the breathless bottom of the sea; a curved arm in an antenna-like gesture establishes our animal kinship to insect species rapidly disappearing.

This brings my essay back to 2020's impending bunyip version of Canada's magazine *Feral Feminisms*.

The Sydney Environment Institute has invited ferals of all sexes to "address issues of the following: animal-human-ecological-vegetal-microbial-geological-cyborg relations." Cyborgs, since you asked, are fictive beings combining human and mechanical life. Their relation to the purported climate emergency is obscure to me but the Sydney Environment Institute and the Feral Feminisms peer-reviewed journal take cyborgs seriously.

Feral Feminisms founding editor in perpetuity is Ela Przybylo. She is a gender professor at Illinois State University, teaching queer and trans writing with a specialty in asexuality:

Przybylo looks to feminist political celibacy/asexuality, lesbian bed death, the asexual queer child, and the aging spinster as four figures that are asexually resonant …

Another of her books "explores ugliness in relation to the intersectional processes of racialization, colonization and settler colonialism, gender-making, ableism, heteronormativity, and fatphobia."

The journal is self or donor-funded, but obviously some work is done in academics' flexitime. Issue 12 of *Feral Feminisms* is guest-edited by Melbourne-based academic Dr Hayley Singer, a research associate of the ARC Centre of Excellence for the History of Emotions. This Centre of Excellence was set up by the Rudd-Gillard governments with $24 million funding for 2011-2018, at the time the largest funding award to the humanities in Australia. From 2018, says Wiki, the UWA-based collective has continued with funding from its node universities. It has 14 chief investigators, over 38 full-time postdoctoral fellows, 37 postgrads and more than 100 associate investigators. The 2017 "hack" symposium involved no fewer than four academics from the Emotions Centre.

Dr Singer helpfully provides a playlist of her favourite songs to get contributors' creative juices flowing. The playlist includes The Red Flag, People have the Power, Ship of Fools (could this be a low blow at UNSW's Antarctic ice expert Chris Turney?), Love Yourself, Queendom, F—k You and God Only Knows.

For the guest-edited issue, the editorial directions for "queer, feminist, anti-colonial artists, scholars, and activists" say that the Anthropocene

> *draws on settler colonial discourse, problematically homogenizes all humans as planet destroyers and implies that we are locked into these petrifying ways of being. As a colonial figure and inheritance, the Anthropocene is articulated as a teleological story-arc that jettisons 'us all' towards apocalypse but fails to interrogate which humans drive and benefit from ecological degradation. It fails to consider that social systems, rather than human nature, are the cause of such degradation. It figures*

and normalizes the privileged white cis-male as the epitome of human-ness.

Submissions can involve "a fingery theory" but even Google fails to explain the term.

While Anthropocene Hacking will make for a riveting Issue 12, the Issue Number 2 (2014) is hard to beat, discoursing over 103 pages on "Feminist Un/Pleasure: Reflections upon Perversity, BDSM, and Desire." I confess to a slightly prurient inspection of Issue 2 and was not disappointed. For example, contributor E. Gravelet writes,

> *Every kinky feminist queer that I have ever spoken to loves Macho Sluts. Well, maybe I'm just lucky enough to know the right people, but there appears to be an overarching consensus that Patrick Califia's hotly controversial 1988 collection of dyke S/M smut should be considered a classic.*

The article appends a footnote which suggests why many a contributor is referred to as "they":

> *Please note that, since this time, [author] Patrick Califia has transitioned and identifies as a transman.*

An intriguing chapter in the index was "Tomatoes as Trauma" by Joseph Labine. An editor blurbs:

> *Using the soft, permeable and vulnerable flesh of the tomato, Joseph Labine exposes the thin borders between pain and sex.*

The issue features a screenplay celebrating the McGill University's Women's Centre. Screen character "Ummni" is authored by Ummni Khan, an Associate Law Professor at Canada's Carleton University, specialising in research into BDSM and sex work. Her character says,

> *I'd hurry over to the university centre to meet up with my soul sisters and debrief our daily encounters with patriarchy in a safe, 'womyn-only' space. Sexuality was our hottest topic."* Words like *"gender stereotypes," "misogyny,"* and *"subversion"* can be heard. *A third woman – self- chosen name Dragyn – is boiling water. The walls are covered with political posters advocating women's rights.*

Later they adjourn to a club:

> *In one corner are foot fetishists sucking hairy toes and massaging tired insteps. In another, an adult man is in diapers, holding a baby bottle in one hand and a beer in the other. By the window, a woman outfitted in the classic kinky nurse costume is leading her "patient" around on a dog leash. In the centre are two men taking turns whipping a very butch woman tied to some hooks in a crucifixion pose.*

> *Ummni (voice-over): Their audacity was stunning. Heartbreaking ... I discovered stark differences in sexual practices, pleasures, aesthetics, and ethos, ranging from the classic s/m leather-dom to the animal-emulating furries. But there we were, bound together by our perverted sexuality and the disgust we evoked in others. It was sublime.*

The edition was not short on supervisory oversight, with three editors, one guest editor, nine on the editorial board, six on the communications committee, and 13 on the advisory board, plus peer reviewers. A contributor thanked the editors for "their brilliantly committed work, meticulousness, and keen expertise throughout the process of creating this issue". The issue was workshopped weekly at FAG (Feminist Art Gallery) with Professor Allyson Mitchell "contributing chocolate mint tea and Deep Lez insights." Amongst her other ground-breaking works, Professor Mitchell boasts on her university web page of recently co-constructing "Killjoy's Kastle: A Lesbian Feminist Haunted House" whose goal is to

> *provoke and pervert. The humorous and costumed characters in the kastle – including polyamorous vampiric grannies, a demented women's studies professor, and lesbian zombie folksingers – give expression to old and new anxieties, creating a space for critique, affect, and discussion.*

The edition followed Toronto's 2014 Feminist Porn Conference, run in conjunction with the Feminist Porn Awards, analogous to the Walkley Awards handed out for unionised down-under leftist journalists. Described by the issue's contributors as an "unprecedented platform" for "audiences full of dykes", the issue saw one feminist stressing

> *how thrilled she was to be at FPcon [Feminist Porn Conference], how enormous were its accomplishments, and how stunning were its alternative visions.*

Other editions involved "interactive praxis of radical world-making" and "Disrupting U.S. state projects of devaluation and disposability." The journal offered feminist responses to "cancel culture, rape culture, white supremacy, Native dispossession, xenophobia, heteronormativity, homonormativity, and other practices of exclusion/inclusion."

The magazine sought reviewers not for critical appraisals but to "celebrate" the works of "trans, nonbinary, or Two-Spirit person[s]."

Issue No 10 wanted contributions relating, among other things, to queerness, transness, capitalism, colonialism, blackness, whiteness and sex work, "topics that are close to our queer fem(me)inine hearts!" Another issue focused on "imperial and colonial forces" and necropolitics determining "who is invited into the realm of social life and who, instead, is confined to social death?" (I know that "social death" feeling from trying to socialise in Dan Andrew's locked-down People's Republic of Victoria).

If you think LGBTQI is confusing, these Feminism scholars have hardly started. One reference is "Expanding the Rainbow: Exploring the Relationships of Bi+, Trans, Ace, Polyam, Kink, and Intersex People (Sense)." Incidentally "Q/WOC" stands for "Queer/Women of Color".

Although past issues have been Canada-based, I felt a quiet pride that one scholar-contributor working on "post-structuralist and feminist theories of the body" hailed from Latrobe University.

The peer review process at *Feral Feminisms* is interesting, given that "peer-reviewed" papers normally count towards academics' promotion, allocation of funds to departments and universities' global ranking. *Feral Feminisms* says, "Submissions are subject to a two-tiered process. Guest Editors review all submissions and select for peer review those submissions that best fit the aims and scope of the issue. Subsequently, pieces under consideration are subject to double-anonymous peer review, are reviewed by peer reviewers, and receive collegial feedback on their work."

Sounds good, until one finds:

> *Feral Feminisms needs Peer Reviewers! We invite prospective peer-reviewers with interests in intersectional feminist theory, queer and trans theory, anti-racism, decoloniality and Indigenous studies ... Feral Feminisms welcomes involvement from individuals* **at various career stages within academia** *and beyond and particularly encourages graduate student participation.* **No previous peer review experience is required**.*"* (My emphases).

Just about all Australian universities have gender studies departments charging young females fat fees for feminist/queer/green-left teaching. The staff have become so inbred that the weirdness of their output goes unquestioned. The motto of my own alma mater, UWA, is "Seek Wisdom". You won't find much of it in today's arts faculties. Note also the Sydney feminists' lame attempts to attach themselves to the global warming scare. If the scare is a dog, those wimmen are its fleas.

The Asylum Atop Their Ivory Tower

28 April 2020

All right, all right! I've been wrong all along. My bad. Sorry. Get over it. Don't beat a dead horse.

I've long suggested that Melbourne University in Premier Dan Andrews' People's Republic of Victoria is the epicentre of Green-Left climate idiocy. I've suggested the affliction peaked at the university's jellified brain with an Honorary Doctor of Laws to doom-crying shameless huckster Al Gore, probably a captain's pick by then-vice-chancellor Glyn Davis, whose personal carbon footprint was embigged by his $1.6m salary package, three times that of the Prime Minister. The Melbourne University's green affliction meanders down to its Sustainable Society Institute, representing the haemorrhoid on the Carlton campus corpus.

The Institute's Dr Sam Alexander co-authored a book with Extinction Rebellion guru Rupert Read who writes,

> *It is just-about conceivable that this civilisation might survive by adopting an extremely disciplined eco-fascism.*

They'd also like to return Western civilisation to horseback. Incidentally, in these straitened times, the Carlton academics and administrators will enjoy a 2.2 per cent pay rise from May 1, and 9 per cent total rise from 2018 to 2021. Suck that up, private-sector helots.

I emailed UniMelb press office:

PART 1

1/ Does Melbourne University consider it appropriate to be handing its academics and administrators 2.2 per cent pay rises at a time when the private sector is enduring its worst conditions since the 1930s depression?

2/ Has Melbourne University since Feb. 2020 made any attempt to re-negotiate its Enterprise Bargain concerning the 2.2 per cent pay rise next week?

3/ Are Melbourne University spokespeople themselves eligible for the 2.2 per cent pay rise from next week?

I got the following reply from PR Emma Sun, senior media advisor to Vice-Chancellor Professor Duncan Maskell

> *Thanks for your query. We won't be providing a response for your story.*

A bit odd, not to mention rude, for an institution founded with taxpayer aid for free inquiry.

Melbourne Uni rates as top Australian university, which isn't saying much. They've all gone downhill since the late Australian war hero and Quadrant columnist Peter Ryan, for 26 years director of Melbourne University Press, described them as "money-grubbing academic slums". Melbourne Uni rated 32nd in Times Higher Education world rankings this year. Whoever does these rankings ought to be taken outside and, er, counselled.

Anyway, my bad is that all along I overlooked the mightier green lunacy at RMIT University, which is Melbourne Uni's southern neighbour by a kilometre or so. I'm a data-driven person and there's an index of the relative sanity of Melbourne's two education icons. RMIT academics, by the way, are getting a 2 per cent pay rise from June 1 and 8 per cent for the four years to 2021.

At Melbourne University only 18 academics signed the manifesto of the upper-middle-class death cult Extinction Rebellion last September, including six at professor/associate rank. But RMIT academics eclipsed that effort thrice over with a thumping 63 signatories, including 15 professors and associate professors. RMIT's Dr Peta Malins and Professor Rob Watts were the two lead signatories, among about 275 signers. (More about Watts to come).

Monash academics came second with 44 XR acolytes (11 at professor levels), and even little Deakin equalled Melbourne with 18 (three professors). *The Guardian* lied that signatories were "leading academics" although heaps were mere post-grad students, and Melbourne University's list included self-described "comedian" and mattress salesman Rod Quantock. His academic qualification is having failed Melbourne's Bachelor of Architecture degree after spending five years getting to Year 3 of the six-year course.

The national roll-call of the XR-petitioning professorial ranks — and remember this is just the tip of the iceberg of top-tier academic green-lefties — is about 70.

Melbourne University sets a low bar for activists. ("You've done the Al Gore climate course? Great, drop by and the VC will fit you with your bonnet and stripey gown for an honorary doctorate.")

You may be wondering what XR's university professors get paid via taxpayers and via their institution shaking down international students. At Melbourne University a 'Level E' professor from May's pay rise will be on a base pay of $199,992 plus heaven-knows-what perks, starting with 17 per cent employer-paid super (RMIT from June: $187,148). A Level D or Associate Professor at the top of the range at Melbourne U will be on $170,993 plus perks (RMIT: $160,059).

The Guardian headlined the XR petition, "Leading academics from around the country say it is their moral duty to rebel to 'defend life itself'". The petition for "rapid total decarbonisation of the economy" itself deserves a prize for bombast by pathetically vain academics. Here's a sample:

> *It is unconscionable that we, our children and grandchildren should have to bear the terrifying brunt of this unprecedented [climate] disaster ... The 'social contract' has been broken, and it is therefore not only our right, but our moral duty, to rebel to defend life itself.*

Jan Palach should have been so brave. (Palach at 21 self-immolated in Prague in 1969 to protest the Soviet invasion).

The petition starts off:

> *The science is clear, the facts are incontrovertible. We are in the midst of the sixth mass extinction, with about 200 species becoming extinct each day.*

If you check the "200 species" links and look past the hand-waving of "scientists say" and "say many biologists" (exact quotes), you wind up with a ten-year-old *Guardian* article citing a UN biodiversity chief Ahmed Djoghlaf. UN biodiversity reports are political documents, with 100 or more UN national delegates having carte blanche to tinker with the text, as occurred last year. The extinction claims were debunked in Djoghlaf's time by actual peer-reviewed work. Life is too short to fact-check for readers all the absurd apocalypticism in the XR petition, which ends, strangely but dutifully, with a call "for the urgent establishment of a treaty with First Nation Australians."

Why do XR acolytes seem so scarce at UniMelb? In recent months I've been to their basements and halls packed with hundreds of XR fans, a great many looking like time and space-wasting faculty members or unemployable green-minded post-grads, and all worshipping a projected image of Greta Thunberg. The Top Four XR universities were certainly all Victorian; my State's barmy academic army trounced NSW and all other States on fealty to Extinction Rebellion.

About the signatories

The academics say they signed in their personal capacity, yet they proudly cite their universities and titles. Their campus controllers are fine with them signing on to what British counter-terrorism police last November labelled an extremist ideology that should be reported to counter-terror officials. *The Guardian* reported that XR featured in the list alongside threats such as neo-Nazis and a pro-terrorist Islamist group. "The guide, aimed at police officers, government organisations and teachers who by law have to report concerns about radicalisation, was dated last November," said *The Guardian*. Within days Britain's top cops insisted their labelling of XR was an unfortunate mistake, but as Queen Gertrude put it, the lady doth protest too much.

I sent 60 RMIT signatories this insincere email:

> *Dear Professor/Dr X,*
>
> *I want to congratulate you on your courage and ethical leadership in signing the Extinction Rebellion petition for official action to ensure the survival of ourselves and the planet's manifold species by emissions reduction. I am of an academic background (retired), MA (UWA, 1969) and B.Ec (ANU, 1974) and am still involved in educating young people. I am checking how and whether I can add my name to the petition which clearly failed to comprehensively show the support for XR in academia.*
>
> *My question is how best to promote XR to students and pupils? I note that Sustainability is a required parameter in all high school courses, which is a good start. Are you personally able to integrate the message of climate crisis into your pedagogy and, if so, can you please advise me on useful techniques and links? Yours sincerely,*
>
> *Anthony Thomas*

Some might claim I've crapped all over the journo union's Code of Ethics. But XR enthusiasts love breaking laws and up-ending civil conventions in the cause of saving the planet. I'm just doing it in reverse, in the cause of amusing and informing my readers.

I was disappointed to get only a handful of responses. But my prize exhibit is Professor Rob Watts, second lead signatory and a founding member of the Greens Party in Victoria. He replied (emphasis added),

> RMIT *Classification:* **Trusted.**
>
> *Dear Anthony,*
>
> *Very good to hear from you ... I have a simple view: the question of global warming and the associated issues (like species extinction) are fundamentally and simultaneously ethical and political in nature (because they go to basic questions about the good society, the good life and justice) and so should be central to contemporary curriculum in both our schools and universities ...*
>
> *I am currently teaching a first year first semester politics subject in which we spend the last third of the first semester addressing the politics of global warming. It worked well last year ..."*

He attached a submission he drafted for the Unemployed Workers Union to the Senate last year about a "Green Jobs Guarantee", and said, "I'd be interested to hear what you think. Meanwhile we need lots more conversation and engagement wherever it can happen. Stay in touch. Best wishes, Bob."

The submission he mentions chants

> *Global warming poses a global existential threat and the Australian government needs to move away from the use of fossil fuels as fast as possible to avert a planetary disaster triggered by uncontrolled global warming.*

It features a nice proposal to solve the housing-affordability problem "by using social infrastructure financing to build a million new social houses" (p4-5). In Watts' world, as distinct from Wayne's World, "not only can governments ensure that workers who depend on renting can reduce their exposure to rapacious property markets, they can also stimulate a construction boom that would generate thousands of direct and indirect construction jobs." Let me see, one million houses at, say, $500,000 a pop, that's half a trillion dollars if I've got all the zeroes lined up. That's about a quarter of last year's GDP – and a million new government houses is just the start of Watts' formulae to build a better, fairer, greener Australia, as he sees it.

His Green Jobs Guarantee involves the federal government as "employer of last resort" handing out a "well-funded" guarantee of regional jobs for all, not just any old jobs but jobs to hasten us to his zero-carbon nirvana. There would be vast pay rises to health workers, badly needed "to provide for the care and regenerative work necessary to mitigate and adapt to climate change." Watt's evidence for climate's ill-health effects from 1degC of warming in the past century is none other than that Chinese satrapy known as the World Health Organisation. Watts says WHO "has declared that climate change is the greatest threat to global health in the twenty first century."

Other Watts brainwaves are "flexible public service employment" to smooth the variability of seasonal agricultural work, and fancy government borrowing programs to prop up hopelessly inefficient wind and solar industries.

I don't know how much more of this RMIT brain flatulence your nose can absorb but Watts' effusions extend to a forecast 41-49 per cent drop in WA wheat yields in 2090 (that's right, 70 years from now) because of global warming. Back in the real world, the CSIRO has just forecast WA yields this year to be significantly above the long-term WA average, 1.78 tonnes per hectare vs 1.66 average, the past century's global warming notwithstanding.

So, since you ask my opinion, Professor, your submission reads like undergraduate green-left tosh and I hope the sensible senators threw it in the recycling bin. Good luck with Extinction Rebellion. And congrats on your 2 per cent pay hike.

The XR signatories at RMIT were concentrated in the Global, Urban and Social Studies Department, with 40-plus sign-ons. Maybe failure to sign was a career hazard, given the solid group-think there. Within the department, the Design & Social Context unit had about 20 sign-ons, particularly those of criminology types involved in "climate justice" and virulent feminist wankery. Science was represented only by about six signatories engaged in geospatial work. This involves remote sensing and ties in closely with climate work and, need it be said, grants.

The petition was master-minded (or mistress-minded) by lead signatory and lecturer Dr Peta Malins, a criminologist working on reasonable topics like drugs policing, sniffer dogs and adverse impacts of strip searches. However, try this among her publications: *"An Ethico-Aesthetics of Heroin Chic: Art, Cliché and Capitalism."* I assume she gets brownie points from peer-reviewers, the dean and grant selectors for slagging "capitalism", given the Green-left mindsets of such university gatekeepers.

As a journalist, I have been a communications professional for more than 60 years, but I have no idea what Dr Malins' paper is trying to say, e.g.

> *Such becomings and deterritorialisations, however, cannot be separated from the movements of reterritorialisation, which are also an essential part of the operation of capital. As Patton suggests, 'capitalist societies simultaneously reterritorialise what they deterritorialise, producing all manner of "neoterritorialities'.*

But there's no mistaking the Politburo flavor of Dr Malins' opus, as seen in bits like this:

> *In many 'producing' nations, for example, workers protesting their conditions are often violently crushed by a totalitarian State acting in the direct interests of – and with the cooperation and support of – large multinational corporations ... The extent of these violences, which includes violence against all sorts of minoritarian bodies (third-world producers, ethnic minorities, Indigenous bodies, women, children, animals, forests) is also often obscured by the 'freedoms' offered within spaces of 'first world' consumer capitalism, at least for those who have the capacity to consume ...*

She continues,

> *Bennett's argument that an ethics can – perhaps even must – emerge from a kind of joyous deterritorialisation or 'enchantment'*

> *is an important one. It is from such an ethico-aesthetics, rather than from ethical or moral imperatives, that it becomes possible to bring forth a 'people to come'.*

Do you get that? Me neither.

In the XR petition's zoo-like catalogue of scholars and scholarship (the real zoo, in Royal Park, is just a few minutes' stroll away), I have settled on Dr Blanche Verlie as the Lion(ess) King. In the anti-free-speech academic junk blog *The Conversation* a year ago, funded by taxpayers, Dr Verlie penned a paean to school strikers and their anger-and-grief state of "existential whiplash" caused by the "Sixth Mass Extinction". Her tribute is illustrated with a boy of about 12 holding a sign, "We are frying and dying. Earth is crying." Verlie writes,

> *Striking students' signs proclaim 'no graduation on a dead planet' and 'we won't die of old age, we will die from climate change'. This is not hyperbole but a genuine engagement with what climate change means for their lives, as well as their deaths.*

The hyperbolic signage was of course mostly cooked up and disseminated by the cynics of the (adult) Youth Climate Coalition who ghost-ran the kids' strikes.

Quoting troubled teen Greta Thunberg saying, "I want you to panic", Verlie continues,

> *The school strikers, and those who support them, are deeply anguished about what a business-as-usual future might hold for them and others* [and many further deeply-anguished by their parents' reluctance to upgrade them to the latest

> $1500 iPhone -TT]. *As adults, we would do well to recognise the necessity of facing up to the most grotesque elements of climate change. Perhaps then we too may step up to the challenge of cultural transformation.*

RMIT University administrators were so impressed with Dr Verlie's word-salad they republished it officially.

I did find joy perusing Dr Verlie's co-paper on "Becoming Researchers: Making Academic Kin in the Chthulucene". The Chthulucene, since you asked, is a new epoch, "where refugees from environmental disaster (both human and non-human) will come together. This is a time when humans will try to live in balance and harmony with nature (or what's left of it) in 'mixed assemblages'." That's the definition provided by some entity called "Southern Fried Science". We learn via Verlie's peer-reviewed scholarship that researchers covet "a form of refuge from academic stressors, creating spaces for 'composting together' [no misprint] through processes of 'decomposing' and 'recomposing'. Our rejection of neoliberal norms has gifted us experiences of joyful collective pleasures."

I, too, felt joy perusing the works of XR petitioner Dr Anitra Nelson, who departed RMIT recently after 21 years' lecturing there for "Pastures new" (see Milton's Lycidas of 1637) at Melbourne University's spectacularly eccentric Sustainable Society Institute. She touts herself as an "activist-scholar", a plus in academia these Leftist days, but once a logical dead-end.

I felt further joy that Dr Nelson's edited works includes a real cracker: *Life Without Money: Building Fair and Sustainable Economies*. The book "is a collection explaining both why the institutions of money and the state prevent us from achieving socialism", she explains. I last came across a no-money advocate in the person of Dr Jim Cairns lecturing at ANU in late 1974, when the deputy prime minister rabbitted about substituting money with kindly love, while his swami-clad office manager sat at his feet, the pair forming a living tableau. Money was good enough for the Mesopotamians and ever since, but Drs Cairns and Nelson know better. Nelson's book announces,

> *The money-based global economy is failing while market-led attempts to combat climate change are fought tooth and nail by business as environmental crises continue. Crucially, [the book's contributors provide] a direct strategy for undercutting capitalism by refusing to deal in money, and offer[s] money-free models of governance and collective sufficiency. Life Without Money is written by high-profile activist scholars making it an excellent text for political economy and environmental courses, as well as an inspiring manifesto for those who want to take action.*

She certainly lets the agitprop cat out of the academic bag.

Another of her co-edited collections is *Housing for Degrowth* (2018, $59.17 even as e-book). A whole section of the book is under Anti-Capitalist Values and Relations. She says from her academic comfort zone that serious degrowth needs to take place in the global north "to tackle overconsumption and conspicuous consumption … The [degrowthed] home is a much richer kind of an environment than what it has become under capitalism – a mere resting place between work." Dr Nelson's base pay as RMIT associate professor would be $160,000 plus perks.

Dr Nelson cites a half-dozen awards and honours, so well is her work prized in academia. I assume Dr Nelson will forgo her 2.2 per cent Melbourne University pay rise from May 1. More money would make her spiritually worse off.

Researching these researchers' climate/leftist obsessions is like prospecting with a detector and discovering a Welcome Stranger, a Hand of Faith, and a Normandy Nugget all in a morning. They signed the XR petition to get noticed and that made my job a lot easier.

The Most Disgusting Climate Cult of All

29 April 2020

I've documented how scores of academics at RMIT, Monash and Melbourne University pledged fealty to Extinction Rebellion (XR). I'll now disclose the real agendas of XR's UK founders and leaders. This gives our own academic signatories an opportunity to cross their names off the petition, since they obviously signed by mistake without having done any research.

A sinister new development is XR strategising this year for the publicity benefits of a member suicide – especially given public indifference to XR since the ChiCom Flu crisis. A leaked XR document from XR's UK "Action Strategy Group" sets out its essential core principles and projects for coming months.

It says XR must be ready to embrace 'extreme sacrifice', arguing:

> We must encourage more extreme actions to achieve meaningful change ... Extreme self-sacrificial actions can act as a vanguard for the movement, inspiring people in their rebellious journey and focusing the world's attention.

The same document refers to "Self sacrifice", "Hunger strike to the death", and "1 person ? Suicide, stock exchange."

I don't know if this means one person suiciding at the Stock Exchange or one person recommending it. An XR spokeswoman told *Spectator* UK, unpersuasively, that these proposals were 'brainstorming', and that the group would 'not encourage anyone to put their own life at risk'.

"Top ideas" in the document include

> # *Scare the f*** out of people*
>
> # *Fear of death? famine, air pollution, placards with facts, roll call of people who have died,*
>
> # *FEAR OF HELL, hell on earth, fire, floods, children & vulnerable people on the frontline*
>
> # *Spray traffic lights black*
>
> # *Hit targets that would hit back harder than the police* [a classic Leninist strategy]

ABC in print ran a puff piece for XR last October, at the tail-end quoting Stuart Basden, one of XR's 15 co-founders, that "climate" is just a pretext for XR's societal overhaul. Basden's goal is to overturn white supremacy, the patriarchy, Eurocentrism, heteronormativity and "class hierarchy". Basden says,

> *So Extinction Rebellion isn't about the climate. It's not even about 'climate justice', although that is also important. If we only talk about the climate, we're missing the deeper problems plaguing our culture. And if we don't excise the cause of the infection, we can never hope to heal from it. This article is ... a call to the XR community to never say we're a climate movement. Because we're not. We're a Rebellion. And we're rebelling to highlight and heal from the insanity that is leading to our extinction. Now tell the truth and act like it.*

Big surprise, XR has been part-funded by the J. Paul Getty oil heirs' $US5 billion wealth. The Getty's Climate Emergency Fund has given $US600,000 to XR and one of the Getty heir's websites touts

XR's work: "The only way to force a change is to disrupt the status quo through legal, non-violent direct action." XR's UK finance director, Andrew Medhurst, oversaw a UK inflow of £2.6m of general donations last year. He discloses that many XR agitators are mercenaries on the XR payroll. Co-founder Roger Hallam gets £400 a week, and XR agitators get various fractions of that.

The other UK founder in 2018 was Gail Bradbrook, who met up with Hallam like this: In 2016 she travelled to Costa Rica "seeking a 'mystical' transformative experience to draw her out of a personal and political impasse. While tripping on ayahuasca, peyote, and other powerful psychedelics, the environmentalist prayed for the 'codes for social change.' Her prayer was answered when, upon returning to the UK, she met Roger Hallam, a 53-year-old organic farmer-turned-civil disobedience expert, at King's College London. Among his writings were "Escape from the Neoliberal Higher Education Prison: A Proposal for a New Digital Communist University."

Hallam possessed the supposed globe-changing codes for rebels sought by Bradbrook (no, this is not the script for another Da Vinci movie). Hallam was busy spraying greenist graffiti on King's College gates and in its Great Hall. He was fined £500 but then cleared by a jury last year after claiming he was tackling a "climate crisis" in a proportional way. This is odd about the "crisis" since the latest HADCRUT global temperature series shows a mere 0.8degC warming in the past 80 years.

Hallam was charged with alleged conspiracy with an XR splinter group in the drone-flying saga that disrupted Heathrow last September. He claimed in court that "Heathrow expansion constitutes a crime against humanity." The beak, unimpressed, remanded him in custody to Wormwood Scrubs prison after Hallam declined bail.

Six weeks later, Hallam released himself from porridge, telling his Facebook followers, 'I know I'm a bit weird. Sitting on a bed all day reading biographies of Gandhi, having my food made for me, is pretty much as good as it gets. Going to prison is not the end of the world." This drew outrage from low-income ex-supporters who produced pushback such as, "Yes it's white middle class privilege. Absolutely ridiculous to think working class people can afford the luxury of lawyers, a stint away, flowers for the police … Do you seriously think working class people can afford the 'honour' of getting banged up like it's some pantomime?"

His post-gaol mouthings have been catastrophic for Extinction Rebellion. In November, interviewed by weekly *Die Zeit*, Hallam said the Nazis' murder of six million Jews was "almost a normal event … just another f***ery in human history." He said: "The fact of the matter is, millions of people have been killed in vicious circumstances on a regular basis throughout history." In the interview he repeated calls for the climate crisis to be treated with as much emotion as the Nazis' Auschwitz, where 1.1 million people died. "Emotionality is the only way you can get people to do something," he said.

XR's PRs of course went into meltdown trying to wish away their founder's despicable comments. The trauma within XR UK was so great that it had to set up "Care Councils to care for individuals, teams and the movement." XR flaks said, "We would like to recognise again how painful this situation has been for so many and to let you know that we have given everything we can to hold it for the organism ... As a new and rapidly growing movement, XR UK did not have clear systems and processes set up to respond to the challenging situation where an individual made comments that were polarising and which caused harm to individuals, the movement and the wider public." XR UK eventually sacked Hallam as XR's spokesman for three months, a dubious compromise.

Hallam, pre-sacking, managed to further befoul the XR nest on January 18 with comments like these:

> *Interviewer: Would you think it bad if people were injured in or by the climate fight?*
>
> *Hallam: Civil disobedience is not for cowards. Martin Luther King also made people sit on the streets. He also knew that statistically someone would die, the fascists and the racists would kill someone.*
>
> *Interviewer: Would you accept that?*
>
> *Hallam: Our activists know what they're doing and what they're getting into.*

Hallam was already on the nose with XR Switzerland for accusing XR 'Rebels' of "environmental degradation" because they used dye to turn the Limmat River through Zurich lurid green. He also yelled, "You will die!" at a climateering audience because they had mostly flown in.

He explained, saying he operated like doom-crying 19th century evangelical missionaries,

> We go out and tell people that they will die. That emotionalises them. Building on that, it works like project management: we want to get these people to break the law. After that, it's just a numbers game. If three are arrested, nobody will be scratched. If a million people are arrested, things will change.

Hallam's running mate, Gail Bradbrook, is an adult version of Greta Thunberg, spouting pure weirdness. In a speech sponsored by HSBC Bank, she began,

> I am speaking to you as a rebel, as a mother, and more than anything, a mother of life on earth … [School strikers] are not protesting, they are begging. Begging for their lives …

> We are f***ed. Humanity is f***ed. It [climate] is a disaster of Biblical proportions. We have to let in that feeling of grief. This is a feminine peace for all of us, men, women and other genders, to feel the grief …

Hallam's Holocaust obscenities were two months after the Australian academics published their XR manifesto, but none that I am aware of has yet removed his or her name as XR loyalists. At the two XR events at Melbourne University I went to a few months back, there was no mention of the Hallam drama.

To sum up XR, I can't put it better than Brendan O'Neill, formerly of the UK Revolutionary Communist Party:

This [XR] is the deflated, self-loathing bourgeoisie coming together to project their own psycho-social hang-ups on to society at large ... Extinction Rebellion is a reactionary, regressive and elitist movement whose aim is to impose the most disturbing form of austerity imaginable on people across the world ... It wants to propel us backwards, to the Stone Age. It wants to reverse the most important moment in human history – the Industrial Revolution. It wants to undo that revolution's liberation of mankind from the brutishness and ignorance of life on the land and recreate that old, unforgiving world in which we all 'ate locally', never travelled, danced around maypoles for fun, and died of cholera when we were 38.

If XR achieved its aim for Western decarbonisation by 2025, there would inevitably be an even bigger holocaust than Hitler's, through famine and disease of the world's poor deprived of cheap electricity. Currently there's a billion people without electricity at all.

Entering today's Australian academic scene is like visiting a 19th century mad-house. Except that it's worse. The academic inmates are top-salaried influencers of tomorrow's "educated" leaders. The Left's successful long march through Western culture is indisputable. #

PART 1

Making Kids Shrill, Scared and Stupid

3 April 2021

Oh my goodness! Australian schoolkids by the million are being saturated with actor and climate hysteric Damon Gameau's ridiculous climate-zealotry film 2040.

"By the million"? I'm scrupulous with facts and Gameau's actual quote on a marketing video was "reaching as many as 948,400 students". But the video was made a year or so back. Since then his total of "lesson plans downloaded" has almost doubled, from 23,684 to 42,696, by this week. So a million brainwashed kids looks like an under-estimate.

The video also says more than 550 schools have been "activated" by teachers to promote Gameau's green brainwashing. Let's update the school numbers by 50 per cent, which is the corresponding increase in "Action Plans" run by Gameau since he did the marketing video. That suggests over 800 schools – and there's only 9000 schools in all of Australia.

For the Greens, schools are the bulk store for its recruits. No wonder, since kids in class are swamped with greenwash that teachers download from Cool Australia, Scootle, an alphabet soup of green lobbies like WWF, ACF, AYCC (Youth Climate Coalition, which runs the kids' climate strikes), the AAS (Academy of Science), the Tim Flannery-led Climate Council, Greenpeace and, I suspect, here and there, Extinction Rebellion. All lessons scrupulously tied to federal and state curricula under the Trojan horse of "Sustainability" mandated as one of three "cross-curriculum priorities".

Speaking of Tim Flannery, the Academy's Fellow has been paired with Gameau on climate gabfests. Gameau has also shared platforms with Extinction Rebellion co-founder and ibogaine drug-tripper Gail Bradbrook and he comes recommended by would-be revolutionary Noam Chomsky and the bonkers climateer Christiana "Tinkerbell" Figueres, who led the Paris climate schemozzle in 2015. Another panegyric for 2040 is from the SMH's kookiest columnist Elizabeth Farrelly, famed for charging her peons $25 a month to build fences and dig holes on her Southern Highlands hobby farmlet. Her take on 2040: "Engaging persuasive and urgent. It's an exercise in what you might call muscular hope."

Gameau, who gets around unshaven in jeans and old flannel shirts, is not only saving the planet but running a nice little earner out of his doco. A US blog-site called "Net worth post" puts his net worth at $US13 million (AUD 17 million). Maybe that's nonsense but he's turned 2040 into an international industry. A US speakers' bureau has him listed, and its clients' charge-out is from $US5000 to $US200,000-plus. Local corporates can become a Gameau "Climate Guardian" for A$7500-$10,650 which entitles them to toolkits, marketing, film licence, virtual workshop, and guest appearance by a 2040 big-shot. In a raft of optional extras are a tailor-made PR movie about the corporate's "climate action journey" and a "Tailored C-Suite Engagement" with guru Damon himself. (I had to look up "C-Suite". It means only for executives with titles starting with C for Chief). You can become a Gameau cut-price "Climate Advocate" for $3900. He claims personally to have a low carbon footprint, although he criss-crossed the globe by air making his film about low emissions. IMDB says the film itself grossed $US1,363,654 worldwide but I don't know how current that figure is.

The premise of his film fantasy is that he time travels to 2040 and discovers that all his green solutions have been a brilliant success. He helps his real-life four-year-old daughter, Velvet, to navigate through climate perils to 2040's nirvana. The movie closes with rapturous music and vision of youngsters of all colours and creeds dancing through a forest to celebrate low $CO2$ levels. One 20-something gal in a white frock grows from her shoulder-blades giant butterfly wings that actually flap. This must be the cheesiest movie clip ever made or even imaginable. He doesn't actually tell kids, "Vote Green", but calls for strong new political leadership. "Wouldn't it be terrific if new leaders emerge who could navigate us to a better 2040," he says. Hint, hint, nudge, nudge.

Somehow Australian schoolkids (as distinct from Singaporean kids) no longer just learn stuff; they're incited to change the world green-wards. Political activism is now mandated by the curriculum. A typical Cool/2040's lesson opens with a "Thought starter: "What excites you about the future" and kids are then exhorted to discuss the merits of "Carbon sequestration" and "Sustainability". Never mind that carbon sequestration is just another ruinously expensive and futuristic "solution" to harmless

CO_2 emissions, and "Sustainability" is an undefinable feel-goodism. Kids obviously will parrot that "the environment" is their future concern (notwithstanding that our air has never been purer and we're putting out up to five colored bins weekly). Kids must then scrawl on their workpads answers to "What is one possible solution" and "Who is responsible for this solution and why?" Thus kids who have trouble solving 9x13= ?, are coached to guide our planetary destinies. The 2040 "Factsheet", by the way, finishes by telling kids to send letters to politicians and join the school-strike manipulators Youth Climate Coalition. They are also to run around ordering adults to cut their emissions. It's the strangest "Factsheet" ever compiled by homo sapiens.

Education authorities bemoan that curricula are crowded with extraneous content. But they have endorsed prodigious school time being spent on 32 lessons about a woke fantasy film. Dig this 2040 lesson plan of 70 minutes – and this is before kids waste another 92 minutes seeing the film:

> *Work through this resource material in the following sequence:*
> *10 minutes – Part A: Activating Prior Knowledge – OPTIONAL*
> *20 minutes – Part B: Concerns For The Future – Barometer Activity*
> *15 minutes – Part C: Thinking About The Solutions*
> *25 minutes – Reflection*

The lesson templates would do credit to Soviet-era indoctrination. Boggle your mind on these:

> *Part C: Testing Out Tone*

PART 1

Step 1. You are now going to create a climate change message for school students younger than you. You might want to warn students about some of the dangers relating to climate change, give them actions to take, or include other information that you find important or interesting. It's up to you. You simply need to create three messages with three different intended tones. [For whom? Six-year-olds?]

Some intended tones you could use might be: angry, sad, positive, hopeful, anxious. Example –

Angry. "Adults are ruining the world that we have to grow up in. Act now!" TIP: Show your three messages to someone in your house. Ask them which message they think is the most effective, and why."

Sample – I saw: – Huge wind turbines with beautiful green background.

Tone – Positive

This made me feel – That the future could be like that.

A further Soviet-style technique pits the majority in class against any child with non-conformist views, such as "My parents say zero CO_2 by 2050 is total b/s". (Dissent is encouraged over orthodox detail like whether we should give up meat or how soon the planet risks frying up). Kids are paired and one writes down the other's ideas about renewables. Then the ideas are "shared" with the class.

Clarify any questions or key points raised by students, including the following:

 # Sunlight – The sun is always shining somewhere. Renewable! [In reality, Unreliable!]

 # Coal – Coal is formed from the remains of ancient organisms and can take millions of years to develop. Non-renewable!

Given Victoria alone has supply of brown coal till about AD2400, running out of it isn't urgent.

The teaching materials claim, "Most forms of renewable energy generally have a much lower environmental impact." Sure, take a squiz at any wind farm stretching to the horizon, and scores of thousands more would be needed for "zero" emissions. I have found no mention of where electricity is to come from at night during a wind drought, although I find stray and misleading references to batteries. Frankly, if teachers want to teach kids about electricity grid optimisation, let the teachers first swot up via electrical engineering textbooks (Caution, teachers: maths are involved).

The brain- and green-washing is having serious impacts on kids' positive attitude to life and mental health. Hardly surprising when teachers confront kids with rubbish like:

> *In the IPCC's most pessimistic scenario, where the population booms, technology stagnates, and emissions keep rising, the atmosphere gets to a startling 2,000 ppm by about 2250. That gives us an atmosphere last seen during the Jurassic when dinosaurs roamed, and causes an apocalyptic temperature rise of perhaps 9 degrees C (16°F) ... If humanity wishes to preserve a planet similar to that on which civilization developed and to*

> which life on Earth is adapted ... CO2 will need to be reduced ... to at most 350 ppm," Columbia University climate guru James Hansen has said. We sailed past that target in about 1990, and it will take a gargantuan effort to turn back the clock.

Kids are even told air travel must cease: "Flights need to stop, or at the very least, be reserved only for emergency situations."

Similarly, "You can take a positive step right now and Pledge to never buy another gas powered vehicle again and get the 'Last Gas Car' bumper sticker."

Gameau says he had climate scientists fact-check his masterpiece. They're all obviously crap at maths. Gameau in the film quotes that "Governments spend $10 million a minute subsidising fossil fuels." That would be $A5.3 trillion a year. Australia's total GDP is only $2 trillion.

The Cool/2040 crowd also spruiks WWF's insane "Earth Hour" which sees kids and adults turn off lights for an hour to virtue-signal for the planet. It's a pity the lessons don't include info about the 800 million peasants without electricity, and the life-threatening discomforts involved. Instead, and incredibly, 2040 promotes Bangladesh as the energy model the rest of the world should emulate. Remember, maybe a million schoolkids in 500-1000 schools are being bombarded with these dark green fantasies.

The zealots throw science and truth out the window. They lie to kids that CO2 caused episodic warmings in the paleo-climate when ice cores show that warming preceded CO2 rises. They lie that warming causes droughts, even after Professor Andy Pitman has contradicted that. The warmist materials cite the 2011 Texas drought to prove their point – never mind that Texans lately have been freezing and flooded.

Even more ludicrous is the teachers' notion that 11-year-olds can do field experiments demonstrating climate-change inter-relationships of food, transport and energy. *"Develop a plan for research (what would happen and why this approach has been chosen). Use the Experiment Proposal Template provided by your teacher to record your ideas."* Someone should submit that Template for a Nobel.

Gameau is more catspaw for the Greens than even a rudimentary authority on global warming.

> *Interviewer: How much did you know about the specifics of climate change prior to making the film?*
>
> *Gameau: Absolutely nothing. I found myself struggling to connect with it.*

He claims he did homework for eight months before starting the shoots. This involved briefings from the usual pack of academic alarmist shills posing as "scientists" and offering their faux "solutions". He's candid that his forte remained the cinematic arts of emotion: "It's really important that all artists get involved and disseminate the messages but also use evocative language that people can connect to." His USP (unique selling proposition) is optimism, e.g. that growing and eating lots of seaweed will make life gay in 2040. He originally injected 45 minutes of politics into a three-hour filmic marathon – one can guess what partisan line he took. But luckily most – but far from all – of the politics fell on the cutting room floor. He still imagines Left and Right can unite to fight CO2. Perhaps, if one assumes Malcolm Turnbull represents the "Right".

Cool's lessons on 2040 excoriate "climate deniers". For example, kids can click on Cool's link to Melbourne University's Dennis Muller, who rants that the climate peril is worse than nuclear war. Muller says, "Media 'impartiality' on climate change is ethically misguided and downright dangerous." Muller, who remarkably is Senior Research Fellow in the so-called Centre for Advancing Journalism, writes to laud our universities' *Conversation* editor Misha Ketchell for his "zero tolerance" against any readers' deviation from the party line on global warming. Ketchell was so troubled by commenters taking his academic catastropharians to task he banned comments on the site. Ironic, no? A 'conversation' in which only one party is allowed to be heard!

The green-brained Gameau has set up something called the Regeneration Group to help solve the "climate crisis", adding, "We won't tolerate posts or comments disputing the legitimacy of climate disruption."

Because the Murdoch press hosts some sceptic and right-of-centre information (unlike Their ABC), kids' lessons include anti-Murdoch propaganda. Says the class material:

> *Rupert Murdoch owns almost 70% of the newspapers that are read daily in Australia. He is the prominent 'narrative*

gatekeeper' in our country ... 55% of stories that accepted the science contained incorrect facts or impacts.

Talking of "facts", the Cool/2040 Factsheet admits that recent warming is merely "believed" to be from human's CO2 emissions, and that dire forecasts of warming are the mere product of "a range of models". The fictive "facts" then arrive in legions. They include that sea ice in the Antarctic is "frequently at record lows" (record highs more like it) and that hotter weather is harming quality and availability of crops and foods. Not so. Recent bleaching supposedly harmed 93 per cent of the Barrier Reef. (Not so, but auditing that figure will get you fired, like Peter Ridd). Plants, fish and animals are scampering from the equator towards the poles. "Facts" fakeries include "Other impacts we might see" such as species' extinction, weather extremes and worse diseases.

The doozy of all the Factsheet "Facts" is that "Sea-levels are expected to rise approximately 2.3 metres for each degree Celsius of temperature rise." For starters, sea rise for the 20thC global warming of 1degC was about 20cm not 230cm. Second, the IPCC forecasts sea rise for the next century of under a metre. If Cool/2040 think we're in for at least 3degC of warming by 2100, that implies 7m of sea rise, nearly twice the height of my townhouse. I fear for Tim Flannery's waterfront mansion on the Hawkesbury.

In a decade of googling Cool and other class materials, I have not once come across any reference to world-reputed sceptics like Anthony Watts, Joanne Nova or Ian Plimer. Rightists like Andrew

Bolt and Alan Jones are sometimes cited but only as Aunt Sallies for kids to mock, while Gameau's materials push kids to videos by "woke" oracles like "Bill Nye, the Science Guy", a mechanical engineer turned actor-comedian-propagandist.

Gameau's material for kids blithely advocates overturning Western civilisation:

> *Tackling climate change requires large-scale, systemic changes across all aspects of society. Simply aiming to reduce our C02 emissions is not enough: we need to rapidly decarbonise our planet. While this might sound challenging, the good news is we already have the knowledge and tools to do it.*

Warmist dogma has been failing at federal elections for the past decade. The green-left's strategy is to use schools as battering rams to get into office. I must say the strategy's "progressing" well. #

Beware, Parents, Your Kids Are Being 'Scootled'

21 November 2020

When I noticed that a top-tier federal-state education body is providing lesson materials for teachers, I decided to take a look. The body is Education Services Australia (ESA), a company set up by federal-state education ministers. ESA provides free supplementary online materials for teachers via 20,000-plus pages on its Scootle portal. No mickey-mouse operation, it's all keyed precisely to the curricula and used in 2019 by some 60,000 teachers, who chalked up 2.8 million sessions involving 18.8 million page views. From 2000-09 this on-line exercise chewed up about $130 million of taxpayer money. Today ESA self-supports on revenue of $40 million a year from projects and subscriptions.

I correctly expected that Scootle materials would be part of the Leftist miasma pervading education, which is so all-encompassing that even the 50 per cent conservative-voting parents long ago ceased to notice what their kids are being taught.

In the immortal words of Victoria's one-time education minister and premier Joan Kirner, education must be reshaped to be "part of the socialist struggle for equality, participation and social change, rather than an instrument of the capitalist system". This was consummated in 2008 when PM Julia Gillard and her Labor premiers brought in their "Melbourne declaration". Conservative governments don't seem to mind that schools have been converted to breeding grounds for green-minded woke warriors.

ESA is supposed to promote "improved students' outcomes" and classier teachers and schools. As we know, our kids' performance is sliding down the international league tables, despite ESA's best efforts. So, as an amateur auditor, having logged on as a "guest user", I had a look around.

"Paul Keating" gets 17 hits, virtually all laudatory; Gough Whitlam gets 56 hits, none hostile and most laudatory. Whitlam's dismissal (1975) gets a dozen tracts. "John Howard" gets more than 20 cites, but sadly none are laudatory and most are hostile.

I got a surprise when I searched on "WWF" to check that green lobby's input. Instead of cute pandas, I got a dozen propaganda film clips from the Communist-led Waterside Workers Federation of the 1950s, such as "Banners Held High, 1956: May Day". Scootle tells kids this film is "honouring the achievements of workers across the world". Actually, a few months after WWF's May Day love-in, WWF backed the Soviets as their tanks crushed the Hungarian revolt.

Scootle's asylum-seeker treatment is straight from The Greens' playbook. Search for "asylum seeker" and the request generates exactly 100 hits and 'refugee' alone 169 hits.

Scootle's intense interest in the topic includes this note:

> *Discussion paper – 'Towards a fairer immigration system for Australia'. This is the cover of a 55-page paper. It states that the current immigration system is unfair to some groups and discusses how to guarantee fair access to Australia's immigration*

system. The paper was prepared by Andrew Theophanous and published in 1992 ... The dimensions of the discussion paper are 29.60 cm x 21.00 cm.

I'm sure it's a lovely paper from 28 years ago for kids to study, being 29.60cm x 21.00cm and all, and about fairness and victim support. Author Andrew Theophanous was MHR (Labor) for the seats of Burke and Calwell from 1980-2000. But as Wikipedia puts it, "He was later jailed for bribery and fraud offences relating to visa applications and other immigration matters." Specifically, "he was charged with defrauding the Commonwealth by making false representations in relation to an immigration matter, taking an unlawful inducement and soliciting an unlawful inducement." He got six years, and served two of them. Maybe Scootle should footnote that?

Another example is a video clip *Anthem – An Act of Sedition, 2004: MV Tampa and September 11*. It presents an interpretation of the Howard government's response to the arrival of refugees in Australian waters on the MV Tampa in August 2001. The narration states that John Howard had often used scare tactics for his political advantage and that the refugees were now to be used in a 'race election'. Views defending the refugees are juxtaposed with images of troops. Scenes of the 11 September 2001 terrorist attacks in New York dramatise the narration, which states that the government used fear of terrorism to override international law and civil rights.

The tone here seems similar to what East German kids used to get. Scootle's explanatory notes say the film argues passionately that Prime Minister John Howard cynically exploited Tampa and 9/11 "to create fear, undermine the rule of law and secure a win in the November 2001 election." The notes say, "the desperation of the passengers led the captain to attempt to land under conditions of emergency". In fact the Afghans effectively took over the ship by threats, which led to SAS troops storming the vessel.

Scootle cites Julian Burnside QC, most recently a failed Greens candidate, who "condemns the 'Pacific Solution' legislation as being a clear-cut infringement of international law, and another lawyer sees it as being undemocratic."

In a mealy-mouthed way, Scootle says,

> In this case no attempt is made to present the case for the Howard government, the narration puts its views strongly and the use of dramatic footage heightens the sense of crisis, reinforcing the filmmakers' view that these events marked a serious attack on civil liberties and democratic processes.

Impressionable kids are treated to a tear-jerking film (aka "powerful account") about an Australian family with four kids visiting an Afghan teen in detention in Port Hedland in 2004. The visiting mother describes 'a heavy gate being locked behind' them, the children 'huddled together wide-eyed and silent' and the guard 'unlocking the third door', with an echoing, sombre and "slightly fearful" sound track. The film, asserts Scootle, "raises questions about the government policy that imprisoned children in the name of border protection."

Kids also get a poem, 'When I think of Australia' by Amelia Walker. Extract: *"I switch on the TV and see wire with children behind it. If this isn't their country it isn't mine."* Images include chicken wire and "refugees' children in detention camps". There's also a colour cartoon provided from leftist New Matilda showing a dilapidated ship crowded with asylum seekers approaching a pier where an elderly woman stands with outstretched arms, saying: *'I know it's extremely unAustralian of me, but I'd like to welcome you to our shores …'*

So where does Scootle offer kids the conservative government's case? A search on "people smuggler" finds one hit from a 1990 incident, and none contemporaneous. Another search fails to turn up reference to the 1,200 asylum seekers drowned after Labor's Prime Minister Rudd overturned Howard's policy and encouraged people smugglers to ship 50,000 people south in those infamously leaky boats.

Among other role models provided for kids are Greenpeace-affiliated saboteurs. Under the heading "Greenpeace takes a stand against GM crops" kids are treated to Greenpeace propaganda via ABC-TV Education (2011): "Watch Greenpeace activists mow down a research crop of genetically modified (GM) wheat grown by CSIRO." They used brushcutters to wreck a year's CSIRO research and cost the agency $300,000. A personable young Greenpeace lady says all such trials need to be shut down because of risk to foods like bread. Scootle instructs kids, "Consider some arguments for and against GM foods and find out the number of GM crops being trialled around Australia."

Virtually all Scootle material on GM foods is of the pros-and-cons variety, with one piece emphasising "Who funds GM research trials?" while waxing suspicious about commercial funding. The main bias is via omission: Scootle offers kids nothing about genetically modified "golden rice" and its role in saving 100 million-plus Third World kids from Vitamin A deficiency, possible blindness and death.

Scootle slaps wood chipping (yesteryear's big villain) with a 1991 report and clip on excess use of paper: "The footage is in fast motion and is accompanied by a compelling music score." Inevitably, Greenpeace gets a flattering mention. Kids are encouraged towards further Greenpeace worship via an ABC-TV feature — *Four Corners: French Connections, 1985. Connecting the dots* — on the sinking of Greenpeace flagship Rainbow Warrior back in 1985, before many of today's kids' parents were born.

Sometimes kids are (pro forma) advised to research the conservatives' arguments but with no or minimal guidance. For example, searches of "Institute of Public Affairs" get no hits and "National Farmers Federation" generates only two hits, one from 2012.

Scootle also dishes up four episodes of ABC Education's worship of faux Aboriginal Bruce Pascoe and his nonsense about pre-colonial Aboriginal agriculturists living in permanent towns. Scootle's material falsely describes Pascoe as a Yuin, Bunurong and Tasmanian man, although he's been rejected by all three groups and himself admits he's "solidly Cornish".

China's Mao Tse-tung gets half a dozen mentions, including, of course, Whitlam-meets-Mao. The others include two on the Communist army's 1934-35 Long March and one on the Cultural Revolution. They are reasonably balanced but there is nothing on Mao's so-called Great Leap Forward (1958-62) leading to 30 million deaths by starvation. China's current supreme leader, Xi Jinping, gets no mention at all, nor is there any discussion of how China has arrived at its world-power status.

Scootle gives "human rights" in general 471 mentions, some involving multiple lessons. I waded through 300-plus mentions of China on Scootle and only four related to China and democracy. They included a brave one on dissident Xu Wenli and another on the 'umbrella protests' in Hong Kong. Ancient China gets about 20 mentions, 19th century and pre-1940 China get about 60. I counted fewer than 25 items dealing with contemporary China such as urbanisation, energy and pollution (including one item that deliberately muddles CO_2 with particulates). Not one dealt with our minerals/energy trade with China, as if our $235 billion annual two-way trade doesn't exist. Although "engagement with Asia" is one of the three all-important "cross-curricula priorities", kids will graduate from high school as full bottles on persecuted Chinese gold-rush diggers, circa 1860, and I reckon that's about it.

Kids are coached to wallow in remorse about early last century's White Australia policy, with an ABC-aided documentary (from 1992) relating how we "tried to fill Australia with 'pure white' immigrants." The wallow includes "Sheet Music Cover for 'White

Australia' 1910" with the song's lyrics, 'Australia, the white man's land, / Defended by the white man's guns, / Australia! Australia! / For Anglo-Saxon race and Southern Cross'. Scootle also cites much White Australia material from Canberra's National Museum. That museum from the outset was a leftist workshop, and when I last visited (2017), it had a major exhibition fawning over the Communist Party of Australia.

On the perils of global warming, Scootle pulls out all stops: "Personal activity — Make a pledge to halt climate change." Scootle asks: "Has your influence on people increased since studying about climate change?" Kids are supposed to make a list of all the people they influence, rather like for Tupperware sales. Parents are to be badgered about their carbon footprint. Consistency is not Scootle's strong point. On one page, 6degC would melt the Greenland Ice Sheet. Next page, 3degC would melt it. The latter page, in a fit of candour, does mention that "it would not happen immediately and it is estimated that this would take a few thousand years."

Kids are given three scenarios about emission cuts, with an obvious push towards the maximum-cut scenario. They are asked, "Has undertaking this activity influenced your decisions about how you will try to adapt your lifestyle in the future?" They're exhorted to redesign their homes for "sustainability", a typically utopian project. Kids might be better educated with lessons on how houses are designed, engineered, project-managed and built, which might encourage Jack and Jill towards tradie careers rather than Whiteness Studies or Lesbian Dance Theory at Big Six universities.

Talking of pie-in-sky, kids are presented by Scootle with maniacal projects like fertilising the ocean by "adding huge quantities of iron and other nutrients to encourage the growth of algae and phytoplankton"; "artificial trees: A machine like a tree which can act as a 'carbon scrubber' to capture carbon dioxide from the air"; and best of all, "Building a fleet of specially designed wind-powered ships that would spray sea water particles into the atmosphere to create clouds to make clouds more reflective." I'd like to see the environmental impact statements first.

Scootle provides kids with (stale) material from the Great Barrier Reef Marine Park Authority. The authority "educates" about "ocean acidification", a non-problem, using a cartoon movie about "Hermie the hermit crab" (2009). The Scootle-endorsed Authority is brazen about its propaganda:

> *This is a highly complex topic and this animation does not explain the process in detail, rather uses a characters [sic] experience of this phenomenon* **to illicit an emotional understanding** that ocean acidification will alter life on coral reefs." [My emphasis].

The lovable Hermie's shell crumbles from the acidic seas and every time he finds another shell, it too crumbles from the acidic impact. Meanwhile nasty sea creatures aim to gobble up Hermie. Little kids would despair at Hermie's fate (close to 50,000 kids have seen the video). In reality claims about the oceans now being

30 per cent more "acidic" are junk-science. Attempts to measure the "acidification" even over past decades are laughably imprecise, corals evolved when CO2 was multiple times today's level, shellfish live happily around sub-sea volcanic vents spewing CO2, and whatever "evidence" is around, comes from dunking acid into fish tanks, hardly analogous to oceanic forces. (For example, "In a lab experiment, a sea butterfly {pteropod} shell placed in seawater with increased acidity slowly dissolves over 45 days.")

Aussie kids are told they can "help the [Great Barrier] Reef in the face of climate change" by reducing their CO2 emissions with new light bulbs, shorter showers, biking and (somehow) offsetting their remaining emissions. Fact check: nothing Australia does about emissions will change the climate, let alone the Reef, as Chief Scientist Alan Finkel has confessed. Asia's emissions dominate all.

It's interesting that in 2013 the "Reef Scare" via Scootle and the ABC was about possible uranium exports from Townsville. It's now all morphed into Adani coal-export scares. Surprisingly, "Adani" gets no hits on Scootle.

Scootle is happy to offer (stale) material from the Britain's Royal Geographic Society (RGS), that bunch being over-the-top in their climate zealotry. RGS asks kids to speculate on

> *How will local places be affected by sea-level rise? Different scenarios can be examined. For schools close to sea-level, lower-impact scenarios of 1-5 metres will still have very significant implications. For schools further inland (for example on inland river flood plains), the effects of more extreme sea-level rise could*

be considered. [What? More extreme than 5 metres of sea rise, the height of a house?] *If there is no risk the nearest threatened settlement could be substituted. 'Create an opportunity for students and make a link with a different subjects like English and look at geographical data in literature, perhaps excerpts from a novel such Richard Doyle's Flood [2002] which anticipates a serious event for London and tells of a worse [sic] case scenario of inundation in the capital. Whilst this is not a scientific book it does make some predictions that may not be commonly anticipated."*

'As any fule kno' (quoting Nigel Molesworth), the IPCC sea-level-rise estimate for 2100 is only from 61cm to 110cm, and that's a scenario from computer scenarios tailored to pump up the scare.

The "1-5 metres" doesn't seem a typo (e.g., for 1.5m); the author is just an idiot and abuser of schoolkids trust. For what it's worth (zero), here's the recommended novel *Flood* and its "geographical data" (so useful for geography teaching):

Can fifty feet high gates be overwhelmed by a wave? Then there is an explosion the size of a small Hiroshima: a supertanker is ablaze in the estuary and most of the Essex petrochemical works are going up with it. The Thames catches fire and the wall of fire and water thunders towards Britain's capital. This is the story of what happens next, and the desperate attempts to save the capital from destruction.

Even more ludicrously — indeed, reprehensibly — RGS material frightens kids with the 2004 *Day after Tomorrow* horror movie, which posits climate-change causing the warm North Atlantic conveyor currents to stall, plunging Britain and Europe into an Ice Age. *"This scenario shows the implicit connectedness of human and physical processes on the planet,"* the RGS writes, which Scootle dutifully passes along without question.

RGS refers kids to the British Royal Society's paper of 2005 (yes 2005), *Guide to facts and fictions about climate change*. It ignores the 43 Royal Society fellows who revolted over that paper being issued in their names and forced the Society to issue a revised paper with less activism and more uncertainties. Typical of Scootle's erratic content, a search on "Australian Academy of Science" fails to turn up mention of that green-left body's primers on global warming of 2010 and 2015. At least those primers look scientific, even if the AAS believes computer models' output is "compelling evidence" of global warming.

Scootle shoves at kids aged 9 to 11 (no kidding) a Jackie French book

> about the possibilities from the greener world of tomorrow ... where the future is filled with environmental hope — and practical solutions, such as common usage of solar and wind power. Lively, fun and positive, this book ... shows them that a lot of environmental solutions are simple and relatively easy to put in place.

Actually, Australian taxpayers are subsidising green energy to the tune of $13 billion a year, but that's a bit advanced for Grade 3 kids.

You may be curious by now about Scootle's parent, Education Services Australia (ESA), as a Melbourne-based woke outfit. Apart from disseminating Stasi-style facts, ESA's been rolling out an online version of kids' NAPLAN testing. The teachers' unions detest any measures to make teachers accountable, but unions' description of ESA's 2018 NAPLAN rollout as a 'debacle' and the 2019 NAPLAN roll-out as a 'disaster' seem close to the mark. Mercifully for ESA, COVID-19 scotched further rollout this year.

From chief executive Andrew Smith's 2018-19 report:

> *The second transition year to NAPLAN Online saw over 2.17 million tests successfully completed by 670,000 students using the assessment platform infrastructure. ESA is proud to play a significant role in delivering these adaptive tests, which students find more engaging, and which provide richer data that helps teachers tailor their teaching to student needs.*
>
> *The first day of testing saw the disruption of many student test sessions. The cause of the incident is within ESA's responsibilities and we sincerely regret the distress caused. I commend our staff for their calm and systematic handling of the incident on the day, their ability to keep focused on delivering a successful assessment program for the remainder of the testing period, and their work and resolve to avoid a recurrence of the issue.*

The fortitude of Mr Smith's 120 staff may stem from ESA's unique conditions of employment. Apart from "competitive remuneration", staff enjoy

> *regular fruit supply, fun activities and competitions [sack races?], and much more — all aimed at building a culture*

PART 1

supportive of healthy lifestyle choices.

Maybe a banana diet is augmented by rotten tomatoes from the NAPLAN users.

Notwithstanding its sedentary workplace, ESA remains convulsed by efforts to curb its own CO_2 emissions. Last year it tracked emissions from 3,678km of staff commutes by car and public transport to work. All staff have been provided with a personal keep-cup for coffee. Recycling facilities are on hand for Expressi coffee capsules, dental floss containers and contact lens packs. Sadly, these savings pale before the team's 666,364 km of CO_2-spewing air trips for vital meetings.

ESA's carbon-neutrality tickets have been won by carbon offsets supporting things like the Guohua Wulate Zhonggi and Hebei Chongli wind farms in China. Talking of China, its emissions of 13 billion tonnes CO_2-equivalent rather swamps ESA's emissions of 824 tonnes last year. But I guess every recycling of a contact lens pack helps save the planet.

ESA's report is seriously unhelpful about its top people's pay. All we learn is that combined, they pocketed $2.008m.#

The Australian Academy of Drama Queens

30 April 2021

The green-left Australian Academy of Science has produced another outburst of climate doomism: "The risks to Australia of a 3 degC warmer world."

Nearly 50 years ago the same Academy was assessing the risks to Australia of a cooling world that climate scientists feared might nip crops and leave us shivering under our doonas. Who'd claim there aren't fashions in science?

Last March's Academy report opens and closes with scary pics of a fire-blackened expanse of bushland. It's a vanity project with the authors citing their own works multiple times, especially chair Ove Hoegh-Guldberg (16 self-citations), Mark Howden (11 times) Lesley Hughes (10 times), Will Steffen (10 times), and David Karoly and John Church (8 times). Even Sarah Perkins-Kilpatrick, who is supposed to be reviewing the document, is reviewing herself as she's cited seven times in the references. Reviewer Jason Evans is cited nine times. Another reviewer is Martin Rice, who works for Tim Flannery's propaganda outfit Climate Council, and features only four times in the body of the report.

Perkins-Kilpatrick is convinced by her climate models that warming is turbo-charging everything (but apparently not our cool summer of 2020-21, nor the current deep freeze in the Northern Hemisphere). She's so confident about the modelling that she'll mortgage her house and happily bet her kids' lives on it. I will necessarily win this bet as the RCPs (Representative Modelling Pathways or official scenarios) that she uses are discredited and climate models have overshot actual warming to date by a factor of at least two. I'll enjoy her house but I promise not to slay her kids.

The above-mentioned Will Steffen's co-authored piece on "climate tipping points", was headlined, "The growing threat of abrupt and irreversible climate changes must compel political and economic action on emissions."

The *Nature* paper included political rodomontade like: *"In our view, the consideration of tipping points helps to define that we are in a climate emergency and strengthens this year's chorus of calls for urgent climate action — from schoolchildren to scientists, cities and countries."*

The Australian Academy's 3deg scare paper in March also co-authored by Steffen draws on that Steffen et al *Nature* article.

Five months after the Nature paper was published, Nature had to grovel horrifically because the seven apex climate scientists had screwed up. Here's the grovel – try to restrain your mirth:

> **Correction 09 April 2020**: *The figure 'Too close for comfort' in this Comment incorrectly synthesized and interpreted data from the IPCC. The graph labelled the temperatures as absolute, rather than rises; misrepresented the levels of risk; misinterpreted data as coming from a 2007 IPCC report; extrapolated the focus of a 2018 report; and was not clear about the specific sources of the data. The graphic has been extensively modified online to correct these errors.*

Mercifully, Hoegh-Guldberg, Steffen et al have pasted the corrected graphic into their Academy report, not the FUBAR version. Maybe climate science isn't so "irrefutable" after all.

Just in case, the Academy has given itself a free card to exaggerate and scaremonger: "We adopted the precautionary principle: if a potentially damaging effect cannot be ruled out, it needs to be taken seriously."

The Academy's authors failed to heed the devastating critique of their scenario methods in a paper last May led by Roger Pielke of University of Colorado, titled *Systemic Misuse of Scenarios in Climate Research and Assessment*.

The Academy paper has about 20 mentions of official but discredited scenario RCP8.5 and about 50 mentions of other RCP scenarios. Typical: "RCP8.5 assumes little mitigation of greenhouse gas emissions and is associated with global warming of 4°c or more above pre-industrial levels by 2100. Up to now, anthropogenic emissions have tracked the RCP8.5 pathway most closely…"

Graphics misleadingly show the various scenarios as consistent and comparable. And RCP8.5 is used in the body of the report to imagine horrible warming outcomes, e.g. hailstorms, p32.

Pielke, who is not a climate sceptic, says that at worst, the extreme and implausible projections of RCP8.5 are touted as "business as usual". He wrote: "The misuse of scenarios in climate research means that much of what we think we know about our collective climate future may be incomplete, myopic or even misleading or wrong, and as such, 'uncomfortable knowledge'." He tracked 4,500 scientific papers misusing the most extreme scenario RCP8.5. The dud scenario featured in 16,800 scholarly articles since 2010. In January-February 2020 alone, more than 1300 studies quoted RCP8.5, at the rate of about 20 per day, with serious misuse at the rate of two studies per day.

> *The consequences of RCP scenario misuse include a myopic perspective on alternative futures and a correspondingly limited view on policy alternatives, the creation of a vast academic literature with little to no connection to the real world, and an unwarranted emphasis on apocalyptic climate futures that influences public and policy maker perspectives. The objective of understanding scenario misuse is not to apportion or assign blame, but to understand how such a pervasive and consequential failure of scientific integrity came to be on such an important topic, how it can be corrected and how it can be avoided in the future.*

Pielke and co-author Ritchie sheet some blame home to the incestuous connections among prominent climate scientists. "The IPCC scenario process has been led by a small group of academics for more than a decade, and decisions made by this small community have profoundly shaped the scientific literature and correspondingly, how the media and policy communities interpret the issue of climate change."

The Academy paper with its incestuous group of self-citing authors-cum-IPCC-contributors could be a case in point.

Their chair Hoegh-Guldberg is a climate activist *par excellence.*

As the ABC put it in a fawning interview in 2009, "Hoegh-Guldberg's work has been embraced by the likes of Al Gore and David Attenborough" and "his mission now is to travel the globe as he fights to raise awareness of what we stand to lose."

He's been forecasting the bleaching death of the Barrier Reef from climate change since 1998 when his modelling put the demise as early as 2030 – less than a decade from now. He lamented that his science peers were giving his research bad reviews: "They were meant to be anonymous but someone slipped them to me, and they were very scathing." Climategate's cynical emails of 2009 threw plenty more light on this "anonymous" and gamed peer review system.

In the same 2009 interview Hoegh-Guldberg forecast the disappearance of Arctic sea ice by 2019. He argued with Andrew Bolt: "This is four million kilometres square of ice that's disappearing. It's not a tiny thing! But wouldn't you say that's a bad sign?" Fact Check: Hoegh-Guldberg confused square miles with square kilometres – but in any event the ice extent last month was 5.7 million square miles or 14.8 million square kilometres. He was even further confused: His *"This is four million kilometres square of ice"* means a square with a side of 4 million km to give a total area of 16 trillion sq km.

The ABC interviewer spliced in tape of Hoegh-Guldberg addressing a conference in Saudi Arabia (of all places) and saying, "Let's now change the world."

Canadian investigative journalist Donna Laframboise has provided detailed history on Professor Hoegh-Guldberg, under the header, The WWF Activist in Charge at the IPCC (March 30, 2014). Among other things, she accuses him of using "drama queen language", such as this (you be the judge):

> *The world is currently facing the greatest challenge of all time ... Humanity is at the crossroads. The message is quite simple and the choice stark: act now or face an uncertain, potentially catastrophic future ... World leaders can change the history of the planet and directly influence the survival of millions upon millions of people ... Basically, the future is looking very gloomy unless we act immediately and decisively.*

Laframboise wrote,

> *The fact that he has spent his career cashing cheques from Greenpeace and the World Wildlife Fund (WWF) was no impediment to him participating in the latest [Fifth] IPCC assessment. The geniuses there decided he wasn't merely lead author material, but that he deserved to be placed in charge of a chapter called The Ocean.*
>
> *WWF Australia recently published a spiffy, 16-page brochure* [link dead]. *It's titled Lights Out for the Reef. Hoegh-Guldberg's photo and biographical sketch are one of the first things you see. In the foreword, he says that unless we "increase our commitment" to caring for the Great Barrier Reef, it "will disappear."*
>
> *He doesn't employ the careful, measured language one expects from a scientist. He knows what the future holds — and he knows*

it's apocalyptic.

Not content to merely express his own opinions, he presumes to lecture the rest of us. We need to "take action" and "act now." We need to "deal decisively with climate change." Behind all of this, of course, lurks a threat: if we don't follow his advice, we'll be really, really sorry.

Hoegh-Guldberg's Queensland University biography lists four reports he did for Greenpeace from 1994-2000. After Laframboise's post, Hoegh-Guldberg penned yet another tract for WWF, *Reviving the Ocean Economy – the Case for Action* - 2015 and the following year he conducted a WWF seminar. The president and CEO of WWF (US), Carter Roberts, recalled schmoozing with him on a diving trip and:

Ove showed us maps tracking elevated levels of CO_2 in the oceans, and how those levels corresponded with the declining health of the world's coral reefs. If current trends continue, he told us, we will watch corals around the world wink out year after year until the only reefs left alive are found in a small remote spot in the South Pacific ...

James Cook University professor Peter Ridd in 2017 got sacked for demanding audits of alleged systemic flaws in Barrier Reef scientists' methodology. He's now taken his case to the High Court.

As an example of contested reef science, researcher Dr Jennifer Marohasy has challenged the standard methodology of assessing GBR coral die-back from the window of an aeroplane overflying at 120 metres. She says this is too high to give realistic results and when she has dived or used a drone on the same reefs she's found the corals perfectly healthy.

None of the Academy folk doing the 3deg report noticed that they were reinventing the (square) wheel. In 2007 climate guru of the era Dr Barrie Pittock wrote a 16,000 word tract for WWF headed: *Dangerous Aspirations: Beyond 3degC warming in Australia*. It's full of the same guff and doomism as the Academy's folk who've toiled a year over their *"Risk to Australia of a 3degC warmer world"* lookalike.

The supposedly dispassionate Academy paper makes no mention whatsoever of nuclear power, and just one passing mention of China – whose emissions will swamp whatever cuts Australia tries to make.

The Academy paper appears even more ridiculous when set against the views this month of Obama's chief scientist of the Energy Department, physicist Steven Koonin, who is by no means a sceptic. He expects only 1degC more warming this century – hardly worth spending trillions to combat and easy to adapt to. He says the scientists, politicians and the media have generated a narrative that is absurdly, demonstrably false. That includes the "extreme weather" meme which the IPCC itself rates as "low confidence" – and which the Academy paper touts at least 27 times. The models can't even agree on the current actual global temperature to within 3degC while claiming 1% precision on key variables. The modellers' guesses on the temperature impact of CO2 doubling have not improved in 40 years and are now diverging even more widely, Koonin gripes.

The darling of catastrophists circa 2019 was David Wallace Wells with his scare book *The Uninhabitable Earth*. But even he is calling on fellow activists to revise their advocacy "in a less alarmist direction."

The Academy – its members are overwhelmingly taxpayer-funded – wants to force Australia's blue-collars, tradies and non-public servant middle classes into unpalatable and dark-green lifestyle changes. One example: "large-scale adoption of EVs [electric vehicles]." Let's check the data (the report does not).

EV sales last year were just 6,900, up a mere 182 cars on 2019. That 6,900 total was not even 1% of car sales. To date in 2021, EV sales (excluding Teslas at $73,000 upwards but including hybrids) are just 0.6%. Last year 50% of sales were fat gas-guzzling SUVs, up from 45% in 2019. The Academy wants to push us into EVs via government subsidies and by penalties/restrictions on normal cars.

Compare the EV handwaving by the Academy with the real world.

> # Academy paper March 31, 2021, p70: *On current estimates, lifetime costs of electric vehicles (EVs) are similar to those of conventional internal combustion engine vehicles and are likely to fall further.*
>
> # Federal Department of Industry, Science and Energy paper, last February, p4:
>
> *Currently, closing the total cost of ownership gap with battery electric vehicle subsidies would not represent value-for-money. Analysis shows*

that this would be expected to cost the taxpayer $195-747 per tonne of carbon dioxide equivalent, depending on the vehicle type and usage. This is high when compared to the Emissions Reduction Fund price of $16 per tonne of carbon emitted. This translates to around $4,500 to $8,000 over the life of the vehicle, or around 10-40 cents per kilometre over a 10 year vehicle life.

The Academy leaves it to the omniscient government to fix the "adjustment challenges" to jobs and industries from its pro-EV policies. Otherwise, "Australia will be left with an inefficient car fleet, dependent on mostly imported oil, for many years to come." What's "inefficient" about my little family car Hyundai i30 (price new, $23,000)? It carries us like a charm on a whiff of petrol.

The Academy calls for "an immediate halt to new thermal coal mines and coal-fired power stations" and expects the bureaucracy to somehow to find coal workers better jobs or earlier retirement. Thanks, Academy! But anyway, it cites its own author John Quiggin, "Thermal coal mining is not a major employer in Australia's overall labour market and most employees in the industry have skills that make them employable in a wide range of industries. Only a small number of communities, mostly in central and northern Queensland, depend critically on coal mining."

The thermal coal miners whom the Academy is happy to disappear, number about 20,000, out of about 40,000 coal miners in total, plus of course their household and commercial dependents.

The Academy continues: "Many coal-dependent workers and communities will be better off under a compassionate, pro-active transition program than by simply carrying on with 'business as usual' (Wiseman et al. 2017)." Wiseman works at the dark-green end of Melbourne University at its Sustainable Society Institute. One of his publications gives the flavour:

> Alexander, S. and Wiseman, J. 2016 'The Degrowth Challenge: Reducing energy and resource consumption as an essential component in achieving carbon budget targets' in *Transitioning to a Post-Carbon Society: Degrowth, Austerity and Wellbeing*.

"Degrowth" means reducing living standards like GDP per capita. As Wiseman's co-author Alexander puts it, "And can we come together to build resilient, relocalised economies as globalised, carbon capitalism comes to an end in coming years and decades?" Wiseman's also a writer on climate change and mental health, e.g. "And while many people feel grief and despair about the prospects of climate change, others see transformational hope."

The Academy report starts with a full-page 230-word kow-tow to Aboriginals, including a homily by Aboriginal Dr Emma Lee who is one of the 15 members of the expert panel of authors. (The Academy signed up to a "Reconciliation Action Plan" in August 2019 to burnish its woke credentials).

Dr Lee told a conference in March about living in Country with ancestors "every day watching our midden sites along the coast getting washed away with increasing tides." One of the oldest tide gauge benchmarks in the world is at Port Arthur in south-east

Tasmania. CSIRO says it shows 160 years of sea rise there totalling a mere 13.5cm, or about two-thirds of my palm and fingers. A more precise study put the rise there at 1mm a year or 10cm per century. I had no idea that modern Tasmanian Aboriginals could so closely detect the tides increasing.

I checked other recent Academy reports for apologies for squatting on Aboriginal land, without success. One report reviewing "Decadal plans for Australian Astronomy" has 90 words of acknowledgements to whites but not one mention of Aborigines or Aboriginal pioneering work on astronomy which is now dinned into Australian schoolkids by the ABC and officialdom.

How left can an Academy get? The Academy last November bagged President Trump and threw in its lot with the doddering fraud Joe Biden: "He will restore funding to environmental and climate programs and, most importantly for Australia, pressure other nations to raise their emissions reductions ambitions...

"The [Trump] administration has also harmed **the free movement of scientists and ideas**. Travel restrictions have made it more difficult for **foreigners from different countries** to work or study in the US... Rising concerns about Chinese technological advancements have resulted in investigations into links between US-based scientists and China, leading to **Chinese claims of McCarthyism** — a claim **familiar to Australians**" (My emphases).

What? Why is the Academy recycling propaganda from China designed to minimise the Communist Party's wholesale stealing of

Western know-how? I sought clarification from the Academy but got no response.

What's behind the Academy saying that the China-alleged McCarthyism is a *"claim familiar to Australians"*? That comment appears to derive from a Senate committee hearing last October. Liberal Senator Eric Abetz asked three Chinese-Australian researchers whether they were prepared to "unconditionally condemn the Chinese Communist Party dictatorship". One of them, a Labor candidate for Melbourne's deputy mayor, later called the question "race-baiting McCarthyism." [I make no suggestion that the three witnesses are in any way disloyal]. The Venona code-breaking transcripts proved that in the US, Senator McCarthy was not just imagining nests of traitors within the post-war establishment.

The Academy's climate doomism is squandering prestige built over half a century. Someone there should have run a check on its 3degC warming nonsense before the Academy could do any damage – to itself. #

PART TWO:

THE BLACK INDUSTRY AT WORK

Who gets to be an "Elder"?

22 April 2020

Everyone's acknowledged "Elders past, present and emerging". I've sometimes genuflected to their "wisdom, courage, creativity and resilience" at conferences six times in a day. But who decides who's an Elder, or an emerging Elder, an older non-elder or just a proud member of the XYZ Nation toting a Senior's Card?

Big Four consultant PwC has grappled with this conundrum in a report handed to the Victorian Treaty Advancement Commission (VTAC) in December. The brief was to advise how an "Elders' Voice" top-tier structure could work with the First People's Assembly on Treaty, representing traditional landowners.

PwC spent 5000 words defining an "Elder", after consulting 201 of them in 19 workshops State-wide. More than 80% of the Elders want a way to challenge spurious Elders.

PwC quotes one Elder: "There is no existing process to confirm 'who is an Elder'. It's hard enough to confirm Aboriginality, who would confirm Eldership?" Adds another: "Eldership should be by self-identification, but I am not going to sit in a room with a 20-year-old telling me they are an Elder."

The "Treaty" is supposedly between the sovereign Victorian Government and the sovereign Traditional Owners at the time of European settlement qua invasion. Labor States are gung-ho for "Treaty". Prime Minister Morrison and conservative States aren't interested.

The stakes are high: in WA's south-west, a de facto treaty is phasing in $1.3 billion to the Noongar communities. The animosities are also high: Elders pleaded that "Treaty must unite us, it must not divide us in the same way that Native Title has". Case in point: Waywurru, Ngurai Illum and Dhudhuroa Elders have lodged a 115-page complaint claiming Bangerang Elder Fred Dowling 82, is not Aboriginal, let alone an Elder. Dowling states his grandmother is a niece of Mary Jane Milawa, a Wangaratta Aboriginal at the time of white settlement. *The Age* says the dispute could derail Treaty.

PwC confirmed there was no agreed definition of an Elder, no authority to determine Eldership disputes, "and no obvious existing entity that could take on this role". It says, "Eldership is subjective ... a person may be considered an Elder by one group (such as family, clan or other) whilst not being considered an Elder by other groups."

Queries could insult an Elder -- some could walk away from "Treaty" altogether. Others thought bogus Elders would be outed at meetings with Elders who are knowledgeable about localities and families: "Don't worry, we [real Aboriginal Elders] will send them packing very quickly if any of them young'uns try to claim they're an Elder".

PwC suggests Elders continue to self-declare via a "culturally safe and respectful process" for contested cases. Elders' Voice members could arbitrate. Elders' own ideas for screening Elders by age ranged from no threshold to 40 years, and as high as at least 70. One complex suggestion was "15 years less than average Aboriginal life expectancy".

The Elders' Voice concept was mooted at <u>a forum of 100-plus Elders</u> at Melbourne's Pullman Hotel in late 2018. It was billed to operate the Aboriginal way, and many Elders brought kids, cousins and carers. The add-ons decided their views were also worth hearing. "Carers and family members of Elders dominated that first one. It was totally inappropriate and disrespectful to Elders. I walked out because of it," an Elder told PwC. The need for "respect" for and among Elders occurs 90 times in the PwC report.

Other quotes: "Youth should listen and learn, not speak and vote … We can't just have Elders bringing their family members, there needs to be a fair process about which youth get to participate." An ambitious suggestion was that Youth could "play roles such as making cups of tea for Elders." A tougher idea was excluding youths with criminal histories.

Roles for the Elders' Voice include peace-keeping among 33 traditional owners and "to help Assembly representatives remember who they are." As one Elder put it, "It would be a very brave and foolish Assembly that did not listen to the advice from a Statewide Elders' Council."

The Assembly for Victorian land-owners has annoyed Elders in suburbia and "Stolen Generation" claimants living locally but born interstate. One aggrieved group is the Victorian Traditional Owner Land Justice Group (VTOLJG) who resent the priority for traditional owners. Its Elders read out to PwC a prepared opening statement that the 'tokenistic' Assembly process stank and hence no Elders upper house was worth having. Most stayed for the workshop; I assume others walked. The stayers blasted many procedures, required a minority report and warned they would take their gripes to all Treaty designers including Premier Dan Andrews. "VTOLJG Elders held a consolidated view that the inability of the Elders' Voice to veto a decision of the Assembly may undermine the cultural authority and integrity of Aboriginal Eldership," noted PwC.

Rather forlornly, PwC noted the vast range of Elder views even on routine matters like the size of the Elders Voice executive. Most thought 8-15 members was right, but some insisted that every family group should put forward one male and one female rep. That would create "a group size of hundreds/thousands", PwC noted, adding that some Elders wanted an executive of just two – one female, one male. Incidentally, the "vast majority" of the 200

Elders consulted was female. PwC didn't suggest why.

The PwC forums did hear a lot about whether Elders currently in goal/parole or bankruptcy, or trailing convictions for fraud, humbugging and domestic violence should be banned from Treaty processes. Or should Elders be cut some slack because white people's justice is purportedly so loaded against them? Some Elders said a strict approach "could see a significant proportion of potentially suitable Elders ineligible for membership".

A State-wide Elders' Gathering of hundreds has been planned (virus permitting), but with no screening or eligibility rules. The main check on numbers will be the budget for attendance fees and travel.

PwC has 60 consultants in its indigenous specialty group, which rivals calculate entails $15-20m in annual fees. Other Big Four firms likewise jostle for jobs in this sector. Analogies with flies and honeypots come to mind. Heaven knows what PwC charged for its 35,000-word report, but it was hard-earned. The consultants urged safe spaces where Elders can disagree. At times the PwC crowd must have wanted safe spaces of their own. #

The White Privilege of Being Black

1 December 2020

Between the 2011 and 2016 censuses, 129,649 people "newly identified" as Aboriginal. There might be up-to-date figures after the 2021 census. Aboriginality is so popular that I imagine newly-identifying is continuing or accelerating. Some academics think so too.

New Identifiers' motives have never been seriously examined. The first published study was by Watt and Kowal 2018, and that involved only 33 New Identifiers.

Many New Identifiers gain profound benefit from re-connecting with their Aboriginality. Many were separated from their heritage two or three generations back, largely for welfare and education reasons, and traumatised by the loss of family. Other New Identifiers are whites who persist although they cannot point to any Aboriginal ancestor. The most famous of these currently is Dark Emu author Bruce Pascoe, who told the New York Times enigmatically last August that he was both "solidly Cornish" and "solidly Aboriginal".

Woke folk take to Aboriginality like ducks to water, or should that be chooks? Here's one case study from a 1996 Griffith MA thesis by Fiona Noble (p36):

> *I was just different, really different, in that all the animals were my friends and I used to spend hours in the chook yard talking to*

my chooks, because like they were the only ones who understood anything that I was feeling or that I was thinking, but I felt very isolated and lonely growing up and always in my whole life just searching and wondering who I was.

Compared with Australia, in NZ there has been much less contribution to Maori population from New Identifiers. And in the US and Canada, New Identifiers have to overcome major legal and social barriers, with native organisations calling the newcomers gold-diggers, ethnic frauds, culture-vultures, "pretendians", New Age poseurs, cultists and wannabes. A classic case is Senator Elizabeth 'Pocahontas' Warren (Democrat, Massachusetts), who got a career leg-up and much kudos for her claimed Cherokee ancestry, until DNA testing suggested she was from 0.097% to 0.156% American Indian, about the same as Americans generally. Her great-grandfather was not a Cherokee as she claimed. but a white man who boasted of shooting a Cherokee. An equally famous US case is Rachel Dolezal, who became president of a Washington office of the National Association for the Advancement of Colored People and an instructor of Africana studies at Eastern Washington University. Her two white parents outed her in 2015.

This essay is in three phases. It first covers the Australian data based on an ANU study by Nicholas Biddle and Francis Markham, then explores the Watt and Kowal material, and then looks at how Australian life can be viewed through a racial lens, as illustrated by Professor Kowal herself.

There are good reasons why New Identifiers are a hot-potato topic, in white and Aboriginal society alike. For example, in Tasmania the Aboriginal population soared from 671 in 1971 to 19,625 in 2016. Long-established Tasmanian Aboriginals claim they're being overrun by New Identifiers with specious genealogies.

The New Identifiers are concentrated in Australia's urban south-east, and the workings of federal-state tax formulas drain funds from the Northern Territory, where Aboriginal disadvantage is extreme. In NSW and Victoria, some New Identifiers are mopping up cushy government-funded jobs reserved for Aborigines.

The more healthy, educated and well-off New Identifiers are also making the "Closing the Gap" data look better than the reality of outback Aboriginal life. New Identifiers in the south-east get official encouragement and plaudits from the woke community on the basis that Aboriginal links were broken in the "Stolen Generations" era. Moreover, challenging a New Identifier is a dangerous move. For example, university or public service bureaucrats who deal with Aboriginal applicants for places or privileges could be deemed racist and have their careers cancelled if they require evidence from the applicants about their Aboriginality.

From the ANU study, the 129,649 New Identifiers at 2016 were somewhat offset by 45,042 Aborigines (at 2011) doing the opposite – citing themselves as white in 2016. The net number of at least 84,607 was still greater than from natural increase and equal to 13.7 per cent of the 2011 Aboriginal population. Assessing flows of "New Identifiers" in 2016 shows the highest number and rate in the babies-to-age-15 group – 17 per cent vs the 14 per cent total. The flow falls among adults but rises slightly among those over 65.

Nearly all New Identifiers hail from the cities and regions – only 3507 were from remote Australia. Victoria, ACT and NSW were over-represented and WA and NT under-represented.

New Identifiers in 2016 had higher living standards than the always-Aboriginal. Their employment rate was 60 per cent vs about 50 per cent for traditionals. The Prime Minister's Department in 2018 failed to allow for this and claimed Aboriginal employment was slightly improving. In fact employment rates for traditional Aboriginals actually fell from 2011-16.

The ANU authors say there is no evidence from the data that identifying as Aboriginal leads to the claimants becoming better off. In fact their employment fell slightly. The motivation seems instead to relate to social and family reasons, they say: "In no way do we suggest that there should be any intervention to reduce identification change – on the contrary, to the extent that a reluctance to identify is due to discrimination, this should be seen as a positive development."

Deakin researchers Elizabeth Watt and Emma Kowal say other researchers are reluctant to explore the New Identifier phenomenon lest deplorables like Andrew Bolt and his racist or "mean-spirited" followers make hay with the findings. The comment is interesting as I thought academics bravely pursued truth whatever the consequences. Bolt was successfully taken to court by nine fair-skinned Aboriginals in 2011 under S18C of the Racial Discrimination Act. They claimed Bolt had argued they "were not genuinely Aboriginal and were pretending to be Aboriginal so they could access benefits that are available to Aboriginal people."

Judge Mordy Bromberg also banned republication of Bolt's articles, and the ban continues to this day.

One of the nine fair-skinned Aboriginals was artist Bindi Cole who announced seven years later:

> *One of my identities is Aboriginal. I can't stop thinking Aboriginal. I am what I am. But when I made this my sole identity it was confusing because I am also white so I was both Aboriginal victim and white oppressor. And then being female I was oppressed by the patriarchy. It was always kinds of ways of identifying that meant I was victim to so many different things that I didn't actually have to take any responsibility whatsoever for myself or my behaviours. I could constantly blame everything and everyone else.*

She continued that her role in the Bolt 18c court case was her first exposure to conservative ideas after life lived in a leftist bubble where she could be a social justice warrior and virtue signaller, constantly looking down intolerantly on all others with different views: "The more I read the more I realised I had been on the wrong side."

Anyway Watt/Kowal say that some of the stories from New

Identifiers collected in their article would no doubt provide fodder for Bolt and his followers. "While taking this risk seriously, however, we strongly feel that the fear of conservative co-option should not deter research conducted with respect, quality scholarship and in good faith."

The Watt/Kowal paper looks at motives from interviews of 33 New Identifiers. Eleven interviews were by Fiona Noble in the unpublished Master's thesis at Griffith University way back in 1996. Noble had an inside track as she herself late in life thought she had Aboriginal ancestry and recruited informants through her own group of "Brisbane inner city 'alternative' and feminist communities" (Watt/Kowal p66). Watt/Kowal say social trends

> have created an environment where people are encouraged to both 'choose' their own ethnic identity and to experience this chosen identity as given, essential and fixed. Our research also affirms North American findings that, for those making this choice, White identities have lost appeal relative to Indigenous identities because of wider awareness of colonial injustice, an increased emphasis on autochthony, and the rise of environmentalism and holistic spiritualism.

Watt says she has Scottish-German origins and Kowal, Polish-Jewish. They write,

> Both authors are female anthropologists who identify as White Australians ... but whose research has focused on Indigenous issues... Some may take the view that, as non-indigenous people, we should not pursue research on the sensitive topic of Indigenous identification – or, for that matter, any topic relating to Indigenous

> *people. However, we believe that empirically-informed discussions about this subject will be useful to Indigenous communities that are currently dealing with its implications. We also intend to address the vacuum in Australia's broader public debate surrounding this issue: a vacuum that has been readily filled with the polemical voices of right-wing commentators.*

Take "right-wing commentators" as a reference to Andrew Bolt and Pauline Hanson.

A Queensland interviewee said: "We're talking about what's the oldest culture on this planet. We still have genetic memory." A NSW woman believed she was a product of her grandmother's affair with an Indigenous man, and used similar language: "Heritage is something that runs in your blood. It's not necessarily how your skin comes out all the time either, how you look. It's in your DNA down deep in there somewhere". A third spoke of Indigenous ancestry as the "spark" or "consciousness" within their body, stressing: "You can't get it out of your system. If you're an Aboriginal, you're an Aboriginal."

Many "always felt different" from White Australians. One interviewee, who was told when she was 15 that her great grandmother was an Indigenous woman, described how she grew up in a "sort of glorified shack in the bush" in semi-rural area of Brisbane with her six olive-skinned, brown haired siblings, and never felt at home among the "blond, blue eyed girls" who lived "in a brick house, with carpet and a carport" and were "sleek and shiny".

Some cited life-long connections to animals, "the land", "country" or the "bush", embodying their ancestors. Others had deep interests in Indigenous culture or people. One noted:

> *I have been drawn to the stories and art of the Aboriginal people since I was a small child. Now I know why … Whenever I hear about the atrocities of the past I really hurt deep inside. I never had that feeling when hearing about the European atrocities and death.*

One woman described a "magnet dragging me to La Perouse", and a man explained how "strange" it was that "I used to pester my father, my parents, on a weekend to go for a drive over to La Perouse".

But a NSW interviewee who believed his grandmother was of Wiradjuri descent, didn't identify that way:

> *Well, only to the extent that I ever identified with Aborigines all around Australia. As political allies and friends … [Identifying as an Indigenous person] has that danger of suggesting that blood links you, and I don't accept that. My upbringing has been totally European.*

Another described late identification as a "big farce", explaining "I couldn't possibly say that I was Aboriginal, because I haven't suffered anything that Aboriginal people have". Another claimed, "to stand up now and say, 'Look I'm Aboriginal', to me is like a little bit rude almost, because you've never been treated in the world as Aboriginal".

Another complained of New Identifiers who have been brought up as White people all their lives:

> *They've never experienced any discrimination an Aboriginal person would feel ... They've been identified by white people and then they turn around and say, "I'm an Aboriginal I know how Aboriginal people feel". That really pisses me off, and I am sure that's a real insult to Aboriginal people who have to try and struggle for their rights.*

One attraction for New Identifiers is that they have been persuaded that whiteness has been downgraded culturally because of pluralism, anti-colonialism and holistic spirituality. "White is now commonly seen [by researchers] as 'dull, empty, lacking, and incomplete' ... associated with 'white bread and mayonnaise', 'guilt, loneliness, isolation', either 'bland nothingness' or 'racial hatred'".

Subjects have been encouraged by interviewers' Rousseau-like view of indigenous people who harmonised with nature. Thus

> *"White Australians of a certain inclination can embark on 'solo-dreaming' – engaging with the land and evoking the spirits seen to lie within it. Yet this process is complicated for White anti-racists' because of their sensitivity to claims of appropriation and abuse of Indigenous culture. This tension has prompted many to search for Indigenous ancestors in their family tree, hoping this discovery would explain and validate their existing feelings of connection to Indigenous culture and people."*

Many interviewees began searching for Aboriginal ancestors after hints, such as a family Bible with a mission address. "These searches were often fruitless, but many interviewees continued to identify as Indigenous regardless. These New Identifiers' attachment to their Indigenous identity was sufficiently high, and their conceptualisations of ethnicity sufficiently subjective, to overcome the lack of material evidence."

Some espoused New Age notions. As a Sydney interviewee put it

> *I see straight through materialism and don't adhere to forced social conventions such as Christmas. I believe in sharing, community and compassion for the earth and human kind at its best. In other words, there is enough for everybody on this planet and no place for greed ... Living simply, looking after family, and caring for our Mother Earth for me is what defines my Aboriginality.*

Some interviewees had stumbled across strong evidence of their Aboriginality but declined to accept the identity. "These differing motivations help explain why we observed an inverse relationship between the strength of evidence and strength of identification: **those with the weakest evidence tended to have the strongest convictions, and vice versa**" (emphasis added).

The final phase of my essay is the insights from Kowal about what it's like diving into the maelstrom of racial politics. Kowal is a highly-rated academic who has received $6m worth of grants and authored 100+ papers and books.

With a privileged middle-class upbringing, Ms Kowal decided in high school to fight for "the oppressed people of the world" by air-mailing protest letters and joining activists. "In 1996 at the Canberra protests against the Howard government's first budget, it dawned on me that, as an Australian, the gap of Aboriginal disadvantage was the one that should trouble me most," she writes.

Graduating from Melbourne University as a medico, she packed a second-hand Toyota and drove it north to her new life as intern at Royal Darwin Hospital. She later figured public health research in the NT was the most fulfilling and joined a Darwin research institute. But there was disillusionment in store. Staff enjoyed power plays and in-fighting rather than cooperation; government programs promoted as panaceas turned out to be dubious on the inside; and staff loved to criticise others' projects as disempowering or racist without offering any help themselves.

Much "closing the gap" effort was actually channelled into "creating and maintaining racialised identities." Anyone walking in the front door to the "indigenous" research institute would be smartly categorised as Indigenous or non-Indigenous, and sub-categorised as "community" or "urban". The whites could be classified "red-necks" or "anti-racists", or "white" or "non-white and non-Indigenous". Someone not known to insiders could be parked as "possibly Indigenous", pending investigation. Maintaining identities was hard work: for example whites had to keep up the auru of a "good" white rather than an "ignorant, exploitive racist White person". The main internal drive was for Aboriginal control of affairs: "The tendency to demonise white researchers in particular seemed an inadequate way to explain the situation, once I had got to know many of them and of course become one myself."

What she calls "the moral politics of race and identity" became toxic. A question about Aboriginal pay rates could be interpreted as managers being exploitive or racist. White researchers involved with presentations to the public had to edit themselves out of videos and stand aside silently to let Aborigines make presentations. If an Aborigine's facts were wrong, Whites wouldn't contradict, and went along with exaggerations of Aboriginal inputs. Kowal wrote in her journal, "In the political world of Indigenous health we don't have arguments, we have positions. And the position of the 'authentic Aboriginal voice' trumps even the most eloquent argument, and has no need for it."

She found "closing the health gap" to be a minefield. The health gap could suggest continued colonial oppression but fixing it could undermine traditional, but unhealthy, ways of life. It could "leave White anti-racists concerned that their efforts to improve the health and social status of Indigenous people might be furthering the neo-colonial expansion of bio-political norms." White anti-racist health workers might be tarred as no better than "racist bureaucrats and missionaries of the past."

In another paper, Welcome to Country Acknowledgement, Belonging and White Anti-racism, Kowal dives deeper into the predicaments of Whiteness:

> *In my reading of Whiteness studies, there is no way for anti-racists to act without reinforcing their privilege ...*
>
> *The acceptable modes of action for White anti-racist subjectivities are silence and experiencing the discomfort and self-loathing of being the source of pain for others without seeking relief or*

resolution ...

My view is that silent and suffering anti-racist subjectivities may be appropriate and useful for academics, but they are incompatible with effective work in Indigenous affairs. The even larger wager of this article is that silent, suffering anti-racist subjectivities that don't belong are not up to the prodigious task of charting paths to coexistence in this settler society.

She has studied how white anti-racists act both in front of the public at seminars, conferences and publications, and backstage, i.e., in tearooms, corridors, back verandas and closed talk.

In this backstage, group members can refine the performance without the pressure of staying in character ... For instance, at front of house, the number of Indigenous presenters at an event should be at least equal to the number of non-indigenous presenters—a stage full of White people discussing Indigenous issues is a bad look. Though, if some of the people on stage that appear White are in fact Indigenous, any overt, whispered or unspoken criticism from the audience is not a concern, as any such criticism simply portrays the critic as ignorant at best, and racist at worst, for assuming that a pale-skinned person is not Indigenous. Non-indigenous dark-skinned people are intermediate in their visual impact—better than a White person, but not as good as an Indigenous person. Indigenous men and Indigenous women should be equally represented. The appearance of White women on stage is generally slightly better than White men...

Making explicit this knowledge of 'how to be an anti-racist' seems distasteful in print, although it is acceptable to talk of these things, if somewhat obliquely, in conference planning meetings. The techniques required to privilege Indigenous voices are employed tacitly on the backstage and are not for consumption by a public audience.

She notes that it is often hard to get good Aboriginal speakers because they are in such high demand and the job is usually honorary. A properly balanced cast of speakers might be organised, but then the key Aboriginal speakers might fail to turn up or leave abruptly. The organiser will then remark about "family" or "cultural" issues, getting another opportunity to display his/her anti-racism. She instances a departure she saw of Aboriginal "Kylie", which saw the presenter handle it tactfully.

> The mainly white audience had an opportunity to not react, to not blame or judge, exhibiting their anti-racism. His [presenter's] explicit comments acted to silence (but also, paradoxically, highlight through demonstrating the need to silence) the ideas that are certainly not voiced, and perhaps barely thought: musings about whether Kylie really had a family emergency, or perhaps was disorganised enough to be double-booked, or behind in her paid work, or offended at being asked to be a 'token black' by the organisers, or maybe she had a gambling habit and went off to the casino. Some of these imaginings would have raised the possibility that her absence was a snub to the organisers, undermining their implicit claims to have meaningful relationships with Indigenous people. Because if they did, Kylie would care enough to stick around. It was this smoulder of inchoate musings that necessitated the facilitator's careful words.

At another workshop, a white male had to stand in as presenter when the booked Aborigine did not show up. The stand-in apologised for being white, especially as an Aboriginal co-facilitator had a junior role beside him.

> *One can only imagine that he implored her, she whose identity was better suited to the task, to read out the notes accompanying the slides instead of him when the scheduled presenter failed to turn up. But for whatever reason (lack of confidence? lack of familiarity with the material? resentment she was being asked just because she was Indigenous?), she had declined.*

I hope Australia doesn't dissolve into a hotbed of racial claimants and discord. There's not much corroboration these days of the "We are one" jingle perpetually played on the ABC, or of "Australians all" in our national anthem, which is a bit of a dirge anyway. #

PART II

The Apotheosis of Adam Goodes

1 October 2020

The cult of Indigenous footballer Adam Goodes is cranking up. Last week Vincent Namatjira's crude portrait of Goodes as social-justice saint won the Archibald Prize which, in this instance, might have been retitled the Black Lives Matter Sycophancy Prize. Namatjira was inspired to paint Goodes after watching last year's documentary on Goodes by Ian Darling: *The Final Quarter*. It re-ran on NITV a week ago and will be rescreened again there shortly.

Melbourne's *Herald Sun* has just given Goodes a two-page color spread modelling nice clothes. The writer's beatitude began, in all seriousness,

> The legend of Adam Goodes permeates deep and wide within the Australian psyche ... And so he looms like a Greco-Roman god: a figure of worship ...

Complainer-in-chief Stan Grant's *The Australian Dream*, last year's rival weepy film tribute to Goodes, is streaming on Apple TV, Microsoft and YouTube. On August 28, UK-based Monocle magazine featured Goodes as its "Big Interview" on global radio. He was on BBC Sport in June. In the same month his face was painted on the side of a Sydney house.

This essay is in no way an attack on Swans' ex-star Goodes, who had indeed suffered from overt and covert racist incidents since school – albeit none for eight years of his AFL stardom. He's led a model life, supports Aboriginal charities and sadly, retired prematurely from football at end-2015 because booing in 2014-15 destroyed his peace of mind and love of the game. But the booing does not prove footie fans were racist, let alone Australians generally. And Goodes as urger of "treaties" and Constitution changes is no more entitled to a free pass than any other political lobbyist.

It's in Australian schools where the myth-making about Goodes is at its zenith. Cool Australia, the third-party supplier of pre-cooked materials for teachers, is providing no fewer than 52 lessons extolling Goodes, based largely on *The Final Quarter* movie. As Cool Australia recommends to teachers: "Make sure you can darken the room. Play it LOUD."

Director Ian Darling paints Australians as racist by the usual cinematic tricks of material put in or left out, snazzy or moody editing, and inspirational background music. Meanwhile the ABC has run amok with lessons for schools carrying the same messages about our racism and need for a racially tweaked Constitution. Between Cool Australia and the ABC, kids from the ages of 5 to 17 could be swamped for close to half a school week in total with films about Goodes, plus the pre- and post-conditioning sessions and the spin-off lessons.

Teachers themselves are expected to spend even greater slabs of time slavering over the film. They will also teach kids to make their own didactic (i.e., propaganda) movies about racism, climate, asylum seekers and the usual grab-bag of leftist tropes.

The film's subsidiary message is nakedly political: that the Constitution be changed to benefit Aborigines (at least three-quarters of whom are city or regional-dwellers). This new racially-based Constitution will somehow "unify" Australia. Director Darling and Goodes want a "First Nations Voice to Parliament", in line with the "Uluru Statement from the Heart" involving treaties and constitutional change "to empower our people". Cool's 52 separate lessons implant these ideas. Cool uses definitions provided by Aboriginal lobby Reconciliation Australia to show kids that any opposition to treaties and "black armband" history is racist.

Over at the ABC, its unaccountable 'Education Unit' is run by ex-history teacher Annabel Astbury with some seven or eight staffers and a $1.2m budget base. It "works closely" with the Victorian and NSW Education Departments (whatever that means) on mapping its projects (whatever that means) to the national curriculum. It's currently foisting Bruce Pascoe's *Dark Emu* farrago on classrooms. Peter O'Brien, author of the forensic take-down, describes Dark Emu's tale of pre-colonial town-dwelling Aboriginal farmers as "egregiously fraudulent." As a sample of the awe in which Ms Astbury holds *Dark Emu's* fauxboriginal fraudster, here she is singing the praises of his dishonest book:

> *We are so fortunate to have had the opportunity to interview Bruce Pascoe on Country, helping us understand the physical and written evidence of a people who, for thousands of years, had an organised, innovative and considered use of land that supported bountiful cultural economies. This is not the history I learned in the 1980s or, I suspect, that some have learned in the 1990s.*

> *This collection is not just a resource for school students, it is a resource for all Australians.*

ABC Education's take on the Goodes saga is even more pernicious in destroying kids' pride in the Australian settlement. It substitutes agitprop for historical inquiry and balance while wittering about "teaching truths [and also Pascoe material] in the classroom".

The ABC doesn't spare pre-schoolers and bubs from its blitz. Its lessons focus on Stan Grant's *Australian Dream*. It has five core lessons and teachers' guides for each year from pre-school to Year 6. In high school the lesson portfolio expands to a dozen, and one of the items has 11 sub-units.

One lesson (pre-school upwards) is titled "Teach Aboriginal history and truths in the classroom" and opens,

> *From 1850 until the 1960s, under Australia's various state protection laws, Aboriginal people were driven off their lands and gathered into specific missions, reserves and stations ... Between 1910 and 1970 Indigenous children – particularly children with lighter skin colour – were taken from their families in order to remove them from their culture and people. Babies were taken from hospitals, from mothers on the missions, and from churches and schools without their families' permission.*

The distortions here are horrific, such as omitting the dominant child-protection element of removal policy. Only one child, Bruce Trevorrow, has ever been found judicially to have been 'stolen'. The stealing was contrary to SA Government policy and he was awarded $775,000. The ABC also provides kids with a six-minute video that is even more inflammatory than the text.

Who writes this stuff? Here's the ABC Education attribution (my emphasis):

> The Australian Dream education resources were written by Aboriginal education specialists Shelley Ware and Thara Brown for Culture Is Life – an Aboriginal organisation that deepens connections and belonging **by backing Aboriginal and Torres Strait Islander solutions.**

There is not even a pretence of objectivity!

Another of the ABC lessons for primary classes (from pre-school), is titled *Aboriginal customs like the war cry need to be embraced as part of Australian culture.* This was about Goodes' 2015 spear-throwing dance at Carlton fans. It was an Aboriginal "custom" dating all the way back to 2009.

As is now standard in school practice, ABC Education's final goal is to turn kids into activists:

> *As educators, you recognise the impact young people can have in creating change in the world. All they need is a platform or an opportunity to be heard … Many Australians stood with Adam Goodes, letting him know they valued his leadership and efforts to stop racism …*
>
> *Invite students to share their voice and visions for Australia. If possible, what would you say to all Australians? … Students can do further research about how past and present government policies have affected and continue to affect Aboriginal and Torres Strait Islander people today … If students feel safe to*

> *do so, they can share the visions of their Australian dream with their class, friends, family or community. This takes courage and vulnerability, but it emphasises that their voice is important, regardless of their age, background and experiences.*

Yeah, right, to improve Australian society we need 9-year-olds' worldly wisdom from classrooms infected by the ABC's social justice warriors.

It's the same with Cool Australia. Dozens of its provided lessons on Goodes aim at turning kids into pro-Aboriginal activists and campaigners, often using their own school for target practice:

> *Students will conduct a class-based audit to assess how well their school is combating racism, bullying, discrimination and harassment. After envisioning a world free from racism, bullying, discrimination and harassment, students consider possible improvements to the school's policies and craft a letter to the school principal, outlining their proposal.*

The premise of Cool Australia's 52 lessons is that the booing of Adam Goodes during his 2014-15 seasons with Sydney Swans was racist. Cool Australia and *The Final Quarter* suppress or undermine the contrary claim: that Goodes earned the booing by provocative behaviour, or in the blunt words of media pundit Sam Newman at the time, "because you're acting like a jerk".

The critiques by Swans haters is that Goodes "staged" or play-acted for free kicks. He outed and humiliated a 13-year-old girl who called him an "ape" while she was innocently unaware of the racial context. Then he mimed throwing a spear at Carlton supporters, who responded in their own tribal way. And Goodes used his "Australian of the Year" podium through 2014 to whinge about whites' historical and current oppression/maltreatment of Aborigines. (To load the dice, Cool Australia often omits the crucial incident with the teen girl).

The Cool Australia and ABC lessons besmirch Australian history of settlement by omitting all favourable and compassionate colonial dealings with Aboriginals. Instead the narrative fosters endless grievance and relentless claims for special benefits. Worst is their studied brainwashing of schoolkids, under the aegis of the Labor-designed "cross-curricula priority" of "Aboriginality". This priority is to be shoe-horned into all lessons – even maths: one boomerang plus two boomerangs equals three boomerangs.

Cool Australia's broadest agenda is to undermine capitalism via net-zero $CO2$ emissions, and use multi-culturalism to denigrate our Western liberal heritage – evinced by Cool Australia's promotion to kids of Canadian anarchist/nutter Naomi Klein, and encouragement of asylum-seekers. Cool Australia's materials flood into 8400 primary and secondary schools or 90 per cent of the Australian total. Nearly half teachers use the lessons. They downloaded 2.1 million lessons last year.

There is no real-world evidence that Australians are a racist lot. Among us are a tiny number of nasty and/or stupid racists, but they are no more significant than the odd criminal or Marxist academic. Reconciliation Australia's own survey barometer shows the Aboriginal industry's reputation is declining, even among its own constituents. Asked in 2018 if Aborigines are responsible for their own disadvantage, 33 per cent of Aboriginals agreed, up from 24 per cent in 2016. Only 41 per cent disagreed, down from 51 per cent in 2016. Among non-Aboriginals, the proportion is 35 per cent agree and 32-33 per cent disagree. The rest don't know. In other words, Aboriginals are increasingly agreeing the buck stops with them, not with governments or "historical colonial oppressors".

In terms of grievance-mongering, the proportion of Aboriginals agreeing that "wrongs of the past must be rectified before all Australians can move on" has dropped in two years from 44 per cent to 40 per cent. Among non-Aboriginals, only 28 per cent agree. The bad side of the report card is that 33 per cent of Aboriginals in 2018 reported experiencing at least one form of verbal racial abuse in the prior six months, down from 37 per cent in 2016.

Reconciliation Australia's surveys might well involve some contestables. A less vested group is the World Values Survey, benchmarking among countries. Its 2018 run found only 3.9 per cent of Australians don't want people of a different race living next door (for whatever reasons), compared with 2.7 per cent of New Zealanders – who live with a large and respected Maori minority. Eighty percent of Australians want their children when at home to learn tolerance and respect for other people (NZ 83 per cent). About 10 per cent of Australians don't want people speaking a different language to live next door – for whatever reasons.

PART II

The findings generally give the lie to Cool Australia's classroom shtick. It has no cause nor rationale for nudging kids to lead us into racial virtue.

When the local Daily Mail polled readers whether the booing of Goodes was racist, more than 60 per cent said it wasn't. Sam Newman wrote, "Criticising someone from another race doesn't make you a racist. The grovelling doco by Sharkshit Productions 'The Final Quarter', should be 'The Last Straw'."

Ex-Labor iconoclast Mark Latham tweeted,

> *It's all blah, blah, blah, in the absence of any evidence whatsoever that the booing of Goodes was about his race. Just because the elites, from the comfort of clink-clink corporate boxes, think footy fans in the outer are racist deplorables does not make it true. Fast Forward to 2045 at the ABC: 'Today we are launching our 39th film on the Booing of Adam Goodes, who retired 30 years ago, sure, but this time we have really nailed it, showing the racism our 38 earlier films didn't quite prove'. Always Biased Crap.*

It is significant that Goodes says that until the girl called him an ape, "I had not been racially abused for eight years and it just rocked me."

Pretending to give a rounded account, Cool Australia typically sets up columnist Andrew Bolt and Sydney radio pundit Alan Jones for kids to boo and hiss, rather than, say, ex-Prime Minister Howard or chair of the Institute of Public Affairs and ex-ABC director Janet Albrechtsen. In a lesson headed by Cool Australia as "Media Watch debunking Andrew Bolt", kids are directed to a clip of *The*

Final Quarter showing Bolt criticising Goodes for singling out the 13-year-old Collingwood barracker. ABC's Paul Barry asks, "But is that really true?" Barry does agree Goodes singled the girl out [Goodes: "I just turned around and I said to the security guard, "I want her out of here. When I looked at the person I could see it was a kid."] Barry then runs clips of Goodes excusing her as innocently racist. But Goodes continued to demand an apology from her. "Yeah OK sorry for that," she tells him by phone on TV. She had turned 13 only five days earlier – it was quite a transition from childhood. Barry and the Human Rights Commission virtue-signallers ignore her genuine human rights and privacy after she was shown on TV, named ("J—"), and shamed to the world. In Goodes' words, "Racism had a face last night, it was a 13-year-old girl." Even 13-year-old murderers are not publicly identified: diminished culpability and all that.

According to her mother, J— "doesn't get out that much ... She's only a 13-year-old little girl. This has been taken way out of proportion." The mother was angry that security men handed J— to police, who grilled her for two hours without parent or guardian present. This was as infamous, even by current Victoria Police standards, as shooting fancy-dress revellers in a nightclub, encouraging false testimony against a cardinal or failing to prosecute Premier Daniel Andrews' red-shirted Labor rorters. J— herself said, "It was kind of a joke and then he heard it." Her schoolmates and the town's people could identify her. As a young adult she's now being exposed again through *The Final Quarter* and Grant's *Australian Dream*. *Final Quarter* at least blurs J—'s face. Stan

PART II

Grant's film does not, in fact it lingers on her face in four takes (from 40.00mins). However, Grant's film is more honest than Darling's *Final Quarter* because it gives the mother and daughter a hearing, and Andrew Bolt is allowed to make his points about it.

In *Final Quarter,* Bolt gets more swipes in another clip pushing constitutional change. Sarah Harris, presenter of Studio 10 on Channel 10, shows Goodes complaining that the Constitution doesn't refer to pre-1788 Aborigines and urging kids to support the Recognise treaty lobby. Goodes says, "We have a great opportunity as a nation right now to do something that is right, and help change the next 200 years of our history."

Sarah Harris continues, "Bolt says the campaign could divide us all and make the Constitution racist" before dropping her role as presenter to snicker at Bolt's claims. *Final Quarter* adds sinister music to headline grabs from Bolt's columns, like "Our constitution is not racist and Goodes and his supporters will only make it so".

The clip finishes with Goodes and schoolkids – some as young as five or six – raising their fists to disavow racism, thus emphasising the demarcation between Bolt and the 'good guys'.

Collingwood Football Club president Eddie Maguire after the match rushed to console and support Goodes in the club room and deplore the girl's taunt. But a week later on air he jokily suggested Goodes should market the King Kong musical. The ABC and The Age, which had reeled at the 13-year-old's alleged "racism", both described Maguire's joke merely as a "gaffe". Maguire grovelled, was despatched to counsellors, and there was no suggestion he forfeit his prestigious jobs. "People don't resign because they make a slip of the tongue. It's as simple as that," he explained. Thus a 50-year-old media veteran's extended joke about King Kong on Triple M Breakfast was a forgivable gaffe, but a barely 13-year-old's unknowing shout of "ape" during the footie match was an unmitigated 'racist slur'.

Another use of film's deceptions involves Reconciliation Australia preaching that average Australians are ignorant mugs about Aborigines. The lobby's short film "Don't keep history a mystery" is a rapid fire of put-downs of "average" whites mixed with dubious or false claims about Aboriginals. It begins with a beer-gutted ocker at the footie boasting that our white civilisation invented utes "and has the tastiest coat of arms in the world" – as if we snack daily on emus and kangaroos. (Leftist wit on display). He doesn't mention democracy, social welfare or equality under law. He gets a pile-on from virtuous Aborigines and woke whites. A sassy and attractive Aboriginal woman corrects him, "There is also a bit you don't know. We have the oldest surviving culture on earth". In reality traditional culture died out 100-200 years ago when the old men ceased passing down creation stories to youths who had refused the painful initiations.

A smug woke white person says Aboriginal culture is "even older than the Greeks", implying it surpassed Greek learning. Others chime in about Aboriginal "inventions". They include "grass growing machines" and "the first-ever bakers". An Aborigine eats a pie to give us the idea. (These wild claims about grass-cropping and bakers come from the fake history of would-be blackfella Bruce Pascoe). An Aboriginal footballer arrives to claim they were "the first ever Aussie footballers", a nonsense as historian Geoff Blainey attests.

Another white cranks up the grievance, "It is a culture that has survived centuries of pretty average treatment". (No mention of positive aspects). Their message is that the average ocker is an imbecile. This one minute inflammatory exercise originally attracted a host of angry comments on YouTube, suggesting Reconciliation Australia is hardly living up to its name.

Critics say Goodes' complaints about victimhood looked odd coming from a highly paid player. His late-seasons pay packets have attracted little media curiosity. The only estimates I've seen are from anonymous online commenters mentioning $900,000 yearly. Goodes was a match-winner for the Sydney Swans, including one of the two clinching goals in its 2012 Premiership win. He would have been in the top salary tier. Pay for elite players first topped $500,000 in 2000, and the $900,000 mark was hit in 2006. There would be a fair chance Goodes from 2000-11 did $500,000 or better.

Goodes also had a fair chance of being in the millionaire-average club from 2012 to his final year 2015, as suggested by the following data. The number of players earning $1m-plus is documented by the AFL as 2012- 8; 2013- 5; 2014- 2; 2015- 4; 2016- 6. Two of the 2015 millionaires were widely identified as Gold Coast captain

Gary Ablett and West Coast ruckman Nic Naitanui. The other two were mystery men. Goodes' colleague at the Swans, Buddy Franklin, was said to have earned only $700,000 in 2015 but his contract had positive back-ending.

Apart from Goodes' salary, his endorsements have included Campbell's Chunk Soup (2006), AFL ads (2007 and 2009), and Powerade (2014). In 2015 he became and remains a David Jones stores "Brand Ambassador", and from 2013 he's also been a Qantas "Ambassador", certainly until 2018. As mentioned, he's also been a generous benefactor of Aboriginal child causes.

Whatever the criticisms of Adam Goodes, he's entitled to his views and others are entitled to disagree with him. What is not acceptable is leftist groups like Cool Australia and the ABC using him to batter kids with their divisive agendas. As an inquiry report was once headlined, "Little Children are Sacred" and that includes 13-year-old white country kids at the footie. #

Another Jaunt up the Garden State Path

16 April 2020

Victoria's Premier Dan Andrews paid contractors $1.1 billion compensation in 2015 when he cancelled Melbourne's East-West Link tunnel to oblige greenies. Against that backdrop his new $10 million redress scheme for "stolen generations" is just coins behind the sofa. It enabled his Socialist-Left faction warlord, Aboriginal Affairs Minister Gavin Jennings, a puff of virtue as he retired from Parliament one day later. The Greens had proposed $200,000 per person "stolen", ten times Andrews' offer. I've seen calls for up to $1 million per person.

Andrews was embarrassed that uber-progressive Victoria, alone among the states, had no compensation scheme. They don't always work well – the Aboriginal Legal Service report in 2014 complained of the payouts' grog and drug spending, "humbugging" and family infighting. Andrews' quote for his media chooks read, "We say sorry, but the words are not enough – redress is about tangible support for people who are still suffering, many years on from this horrific policy."

Sorry, but Victoria never ran "horrific" stealing policies and Dan's cited "evil chapter" is mythical. Six official inquiries between 1996 and 2003 found no Victorian policies and no victims. The 2003 task force said there had been no policy to remove children. The 1996 report conceded that a century ago very few children were being removed and, from 1957, the Welfare Board had no authority to remove them.

Apprentices were boarded out (three or four a year from 1912-29) and children were placed in industrial schools (about five a year from 1901-52). "Few, if any" removals from 1890-1930 claimed parental neglect. The 1996 submission even counted as "stolen" 400 young felons imprisoned just like young white crims. Nearly all returned home. Judge-approved adoptions from 1958-68 averaged only one or two per year, mostly babies of teens from interstate.

There were two grey episodes. In the 1950s, police brought 150 Aboriginal children to court after a roundup in shanty towns that included 24 kids living on the Mooroopna rubbish dump. In the late 1960s Aboriginal Welfare officials uncovered 300 informal private adoptions. They strove to re-unite the families, since State policy was against family separations, not creating them. Historian Keith Windschuttle estimates from his archival counts that 700 Aboriginal children in Victoria were removed between 1890-1970, for all reasons, and voluntarily or not. That's about nine children removed per year. Nationally such removals totalled about 8250 last century, for all reasons.

By 2005, embarrassed Victorian politicians solved their non-problem by redefining "stolen" as those separated from community, family, land or culture, no matter how short, how voluntary and for whatever reason, plus all the descendants. And the whole families involved were now viewed as "stolen" survivors. The result, as Windschuttle put it, was that Victorian "stolen" numbers went from virtually none to virtually all.

This was so implausible that a new legitimising tactic evolved in 2018. The Australian Institute of Health and Welfare and the Healing Foundation generated national counts of the "stolen" using five Australian Bureau of Statistics surveys from 2002-15. This led to a 2018 total of 17,000 for surviving Aboriginals born before 1972 (when alleged "stealing" ceased) and who also reported removal from their families. The Victorian figure at 2014-15 was 1341. The report further tabulated about 100,000 descendants of the "stolen". This was a third of all adult Aborigines, including 9000 descendants in Victoria.

The ABS survey questions were:

1/ Have you been removed from your family by welfare or the government or taken away to a mission?

2/ Have any of your relatives been removed from your family by welfare or the government or taken away to a mission?

The questions involve no distinctions between voluntary and enforced removal, no reasons for removal (welfare, racist or last resort), and no date or duration of removal.

Question Two is quite subjective, asking about family lore or hearsay concerning "any type of relative", according to the Institute. Answers could range from upbringing at a children's home (for whatever reason) to a tale about a pre-war great-grandmother who got a trip from her inland mission to the seaside. This survey generated the highest possible number of "stolen" kids. Nonetheless, it is clear from the report that legalised removal for whatever reason had bad outcomes, across a swathe of 20 indicators.

But some results were absurd. About 18,000 national respondents in 2014 said they were "removed" after 1972, *after* the alleged racist practices ceased. These 18,000 mistaken respondents were only slightly fewer than the 21,000 saying, at least plausibly, that they were "removed" pre-1972 (p91). And the fourth ABS survey in 2012-13 produced such exaggerated removal figures that it was binned even by the report-writers.

The population claiming Aboriginality has soared as people choose this fashionable identity, creating an "unfortunate" glitch in the "stolen" statistics, the report says. In 2008 the increase was 17 per cent above the demographic estimate.

South Australian governments also love apologising for stealing generations. Sure, Adelaide produced Australia's sole court-verified case, Bruce Trevorrow, stolen from hospital at 13 months by a deluded welfare officer in 1958. He won $775,000, why no wins by others?

SA had laws since 1911 against "stealing" the children. But from 1939-58 bureaucrats removed about 300 children illegally (including Bruce Trevorrow), some for neglect or with consent. SA archival experts Alistair Crooks and Joe Lane have re-keyed to their site, *firstsources.info*, some 22,000 letters of Aboriginal Protectors from 1840-1912. From 1840 to 1940, SA removals averaged two to three per year, for all reasons including having been orphaned, they found. Windschuttle's SA count for 1900-1970 was 16 a year, for all reasons. The SA government itself has cited miniscule removals, such as five a year from 1909-1913, for all reasons.

The Protectors were so keen to preserve families that from 1860 they provided many scores of 15ft fishing boats and canoes, free or half-price, to Murray River-dwelling groups, along with tackle and rifles for self-sufficiency. From the 1940s, travelling staff coached mothers on child-rearing to minimise removals for neglect.

Contrast that with modern Victoria. As of June 2018, 8.9 per cent of the children were in care placements, 20 times the non-indigenous rate, and the worst rate in Australia. Dan Andrews should focus on his government's current child removals rather than alleged historic ones. #

Bruce Pascoe's Tribe Dines on Young Brains

27 July 2020

The culture wars in Australia's latest decade are personified by "Aboriginal" Bruce Pascoe, an "historian". Now an Enterprise Professor in Indigenous Agriculture at Melbourne University, he espouses that pre-contact Aboriginals lived in towns of a thousand people, planting harvesting and storing crops, sewing their clothes and keeping their livestock (wallabies? wombats?) in pens. These towns were "buzzing with happiness", Pascoe writes. Literally millions of Australian schoolchildren are being force-fed this nonsense. Historian Geoff Blainey says there's no evidence for any of it. So why is it being pushed by the ABC and the Left? Because if it were true, it would bolster the ideas of Aboriginal sovereignty, treaties and compensation. In other words, an end to the Australian experiment with equality under the law. How can anyone satirise a situation that is already ridiculous? I've tried. Read on ...

Sixteen-year-old Edwina Snodgrass-Greencaper (not her real name) arrives home from Williamstown Terrific College and asks, "Mummy, what's for tea?" Williamstown, for those blessed not to live in Melbourne, is a gentrified suburb, now very much upper-middle class, across the bay from Melbourne's CBD.

Mummy: I've cooked what your sustainability teacher recommends. We're starting with kangaroo-tail soup, then roast kangaroo ribs for mains. Dessert will be dough-cake made from native millet and nardoo.

PART II

Edwina: That's so great, Mummy!

Mummy: Now put on your kangaroo-skin slippers, and here's your kangaroo-skin cloak.

Edwina: It's so great that my sustainability teacher has shown Australia how to cool the planet with kangaroos because they emit little methane, unlike sheep, cows ... and Daddy. And our Dan Andrews-run kangaroo industry, skilfully managed by Aboriginal firestick farming, is restoring the landscape that ignorant farmers were degrading.

This hypothetical teacher-led overhaul of the meat industry originates from self-styled Aboriginal Bruce Pascoe and his faux-history of Aboriginal farming civilisations. *Dark Emu* (for credulous adults) has spawned his glossy *Young Dark Emu – A Truer History* (for brain-washable kids). That in turn has spawned *Dark Emu in the Classroom: Teacher Resources for High School Geography*.

One author of Teacher Resources is Simone Barlow BA (Syd), Dip.Ed (Melb), cited as a geography teacher at Williamstown High Senior Campus. The other is Ashlee Horyniak M.Ed (Melb), and BA (Hons) with a history minor in Aboriginality "through an anthropological and historical lens". Ms Horyniak is cited as Humanities Coordinator at the Williamstown High. They say: "Simply put, Dark Emu should be compulsory reading for every teacher."

Teacher ignorance is no barrier to foisting potted Pascoe piffle on our kids. The authors:

> *Whilst we recommend reading Dark Emu for yourself, this teacher resource is designed so that teachers without the book, Dark Emu, and with little prior knowledge, can pick it up and teach.*

Bruce Pascoe is the darling of the ABC and all other left-thinkers because he claims that pre-colonial Aborigines included crop-growers in permanent towns of 1000 who kept their livestock in pens. This accords with currently fashionable thinking about Aboriginal "nations" and treaties. He's won a prize awarded to Aboriginal authors but has not rebutted genealogies suggesting his forebears, every single one of them, were from British stock.

The ABC is preparing a two-part tribute to Pascoe scheduled to be broadcast this year and has already put up a 14-chapter Pascoe extravaganza on ABC Education. But even the ABC has quietly added a Prologue update that Pascoe's thesis is contestable.

In the NSW Parliament last March, the Education Minister affirmed that *Dark Emu* is not part of the NSW curriculum but is mentioned in two sample texts. Schools work out for themselves how subjects are taught and have "the scope to present topics in ways that support the school ethos and the diversity of student needs," the minister said. I don't know the official status of *Dark Emu in the Classroom: Teacher Resources in Victoria*, but it's a lavish production suggestive of high sales volume.

The Williamstown teachers' kangaroo-led plan for agriculture occupies six pages of their 94-page *Resource*. Students role-play interest groups. For example, animal-rights activists give the thumbs down to culling of 'roos, consumers love that 'roo taste, and rather weirdly, the outback's hard-bitten 'roo types say: "European colonisation has greatly changed what was a happy cohabitation between Aboriginals and animals for thousands of years. The commercial harvest is a replacement of Aboriginal hunting and dingo predation …"

I'm not sure how happy your average 'roo was to get a spear through its ribs.

The luckiest kids get to role-play Bruce Pascoe himself, whom we are told by the two teacher authors is an Aboriginal of Bunurong/Tasmanian heritage. (Somehow his additional claim to Yuin heritage has faded out, although still bruited by the ABC). With the Aboriginal Mr Pascoe as avatar, role-playing kids say, "We need to be consulted on [kangaroos]. We have been here forever, since the Dreaming, and have managed the land very effectively until the arrival of white man."

Actually the Bunurong are adamant that Pascoe is not one of theirs, and Tasmania's clan led by Michael Mansell has outed Pascoe even more forcibly as "fake".

The teachers' kangaroo-future lessons end with two (and only two) of what are dubbed "Scenario Cards". The first card seeks kids' views on a 10 per cent increase in culling. The second is a corker:

> *Most of Australia's agricultural areas have been destroyed by erosion and desertification. The price of beef and lamb has risen by ten times as there are very few viable farms. Consumers are*

> *frustrated and looking elsewhere. Is kangaroo meat the future of the Australian meat industry? What should be done?*
>
> *"Points to discuss in your group: How do you feel about this? How does this affect you? What do you think needs to be done? Are there any other possible solutions to the problem?*

A wipe-out of Australian agriculture would indeed be "a problem" unless, say, we buy up rice paddies in China. Kids will intuit that "the problem" is climate-related and that the solution is more wind turbines.

The authors deny that British-based agriculture was more productive than the Aborigines' version.

> *The colonists ignored Aboriginal methods and brought their own, which were poorly suited to the landscape ... We can only assume it was a combination of ignorance and cultural blindness, because it is clear that the land was well managed prior to colonists, and degraded in such a short period of time after their arrival.*

Scepticism about Pascoe's Aboriginal-farmer fantasies is out of bounds. The authors tell kids,

> *You can link in the ideas of this [Pascoe] truth being inconvenient, that it cancels out the very foundations of colonisation on 'Terra Nullius' and the implications of accepting this perspective.*

Here's more guidance for teachers:

\# The authors spurn what they call the capitalist view of human evolution, which resembles Adolf's Third Reich: "Only the fittest survive ... the weakest individuals – and civilisations – eventually die". They recommend a rival creed of "cooperation with, and care for, other humans and the natural environment ... and the preservation of the planet." They claim this caring non-capitalist community "aligns more closely" with pre-colonial Aboriginality: "Modern economic systems often prioritise profit and progress over the protection of air quality, land or clean water."

The authors urge the "more able students" to read a piece by Aboriginal feminist trade unionist Celeste Liddle praising Labor's Paul Keating and saying that ex-PM John Howard's "downplaying of Indigenous suffering was so despicable that Indigenous people took to turning their back on him in public forums." The only other article the authors recommend in this section blasts Prime Minister Turnbull's lack of action on Aboriginal federal representation and says, "Aboriginal leader Sean Gordon will help form a new political party after this week quitting the Liberals in disgust."

So much for non-politicised classrooms!

Farming and farmers are disparaged and I assume city kids' views are shaped accordingly:

> *Resource use is a current challenge to Australia. Our lands are being degraded by current farming methods. Our cities are struggling to meet our water demands* [thanks to greenies' bans on dams] ... *Our current farming methods are having devastating impacts on the environment. Let's embrace [Aboriginal knowledge] and change our current degrading ways.*

They continue:

> Pascoe's exercise goes some way toward reducing the continuing damage of colonialism. This is not a simple task but we can begin by acknowledging that Aboriginal Australians built houses, cultivated and irrigated crops and sewed clothes. Over many thousands of years Aboriginal Australia learnt how to increase the productivity of the land and this enormous expertise is useful to us today.

Actual film from the mid-1900s of some non-Westernised Aboriginals' foraging and clothing tells another story, of a family obviously eking out a marginal existence from seed gathering.

The book says,

> The yam daisy was once a crucial plant in Australia, and, as the population continues to grow and climate change remains a barrier to food security, its current value must be considered.

The past century's 1degC warming has seen global grain output rising to records for each of the past two years and Australian winter crop production this year forecast to increase to 11 per cent above the 10-year average. While the figures post-date the 2019 book, any glance at crop data shows the long-term rising yields. Global warming to date has been a boon to food production.

The book also asks

> Is firestick farming an effective management tool? Should it be more widespread today? ... Should firestick farming be adopted

as a method of managing the landscapes of rural Australia?

Fact-check: Firestick farming in Indonesia creates the vast annual smoke hazes across SE Asia and into northern Australia. Firestick farming also blights the Amazon forests.

Despite Pascoe and teacher enthusiasms, native wild rice doesn't seem the answer. Its productivity and potential is miniscule, according to an ABC article referenced by the authors. It would have to be hand-sorted after milling to get rid of waste, which is why, back in 2014, it was costed at $120 per kilogram. Woollies is selling rice this week for as little as $1.50. But you may be inspired to try Indigenous sourdough dancing-grass-seed damper after hearing Pascoe on the ABC.

How might Indigenous fish traps become a model for the aquaculture industry?

Aquaculture today is a high-tech biological industry, the opposite of trapping wild fish.

The authors ask, "What role could ATSI [Aboriginal] strategies play in ensuring food security across Australia?" To inject some anthropology into this stuff, a tribal strategy even into the 1960s to cope with drought and food scarcity was infanticide. These extracts are just from SA:

1865: The issuer of rations at Overland Corner, SA, reports that in his district in the recent years, 'every living child appears to have been destroyed immediately after birth.'

1874: Point McLeay missionary, Rev. Taplin, writes, "Savage life is most destructive of infant life." In the same year, Sub-Protector W.R. Thompson reported 'half-castes' in camps rarely survive to adulthood.

1924: Protector William Garnett South writes, "It is generally reported and doubtless true, that aborigines in these parts of Australia often kill children not wanted, and especially 'half-castes'."

1960s: Infanticide rates around Ernabella Mission are up to a fifth of all births, according to anthropologist Aram A. Yengolen.

West Australian MLA W.L. Grayden caused controversy when he reported in 1956 about alleged starving bands in the Warburton Ranges, with infanticide being common. Others disagreed. Professor Ronald Berndt (my 1960 anthropology lecturer) investigated and reported: "It seems clear that although occasional cases [of infanticide] do occur among traditionally oriented Aborigines, these are becoming even less frequent than they were in the past" (p33).

The *Teacher Resource* book disparages evidence **against** Aborigines as farmers:

> *When examining the sources for bias, students should look at the author and their [sic] motivations for producing the source.*

But Pascoe's own claims go unqueried. In *Dark Emu* they include Walt Disney-style stories like:

PART II

> *When the natives see a whale being chased by killer whales one of the old men pretends to be lame and frail ... to excite the compassion of the killer whales and the man calls on the killers to bring the whale ashore. When the injured whale drifts in to shore the other men come out of hiding to kill the whale and call on neighbouring tribes to join the feast.*

Peter O'Brien in his *Bitter Harvest* book debunks this and countless other Pascoe tales. O'Brien finds documents only about white whalers' cooperation with killer whales on the south coast of NSW, with the skeleton of the leading killer whale, "Old Tom" now preserved in the Eden Killer Whale Museum.

The *Resource's* text, sadly, goes haywire when it approaches some rigorous material amid its Pascoe blather. A section on correct graphing techniques reads, "Ensure you use a consistent scale (i.e., 1.5cm represents 1 million years or 1cm represents 1 million years). Ensure your graph has SALTS (scale, axis, legend, title and sources)." Problem is, the cited data for graphing covers only 38 years, 1980-2018. The "million years" is quite a typo.

It's disturbing that the *Resource* and much other teaching these days tell kids how social conditions should be, rather than how things verifiably are. Hence the *Resource's* 'kangaroo dreaming' in lieu of educating kids about Australia's meat production and productivity, exports (including the genuine 'live sheep' controversies) and trading partners (China in particular).

The educationists' final and explicit goal is to turn the kids into activists, but only for OK green-Left causes. Kids are constantly exhorted to send letters to their local Member or gee-up their own school principal to make the school more woke. The impetus in all States (Labor and Conservative) is from the top through the national curriculum authority (ACARA) which mandates:

> *The learning area [ideally] provides content that supports the development of* **students' world views**, *particularly in relation to judgements about past social and economic systems, and access to and use of Earth's resources … Students explore contemporary issues of sustainability and* **develop action plans and possible solutions** *to local, national and global issues which have social, economic and environmental perspectives."* (My emphases. Maybe teens should solve global problems after they solve the mess in their bedrooms).

The crowning insult to conservative parents is the three Julia Gillard-endorsed "cross-curriculum priorities" since 2009 which force teachers to lard all subjects with sustainability, Aboriginality and (lame-duck) Asian emphases. Worst of all, "sustainability" has become an open-sesame for every green-Left lobby from Cool Australia to ACF and Greenpeace to inject their agitprop into classrooms.

The Williamstown duo's Teacher Resources opens a window onto how kids are actually taught and what stories they are force-fed. Are conservative politicians asleep as the education system converts trusting youngsters into green variants of China's Red Guards? Or is that they are simply too cowardly to raise a fuss? #

BLM: Black Landlords Matter

19 April 2021

Some of us, or lefties anyway, imagine Black Lives Matter (BLM) to be a charity something like the Red Cross or Brotherhood of St Laurence but without the op shops, its founders akin to Florence Nightingale or Albert Schweizer. As Wikipedia puts it with a typical Left narrative slant, "The movement comprises many views and a broad array of demands but they centre on criminal justice reform."

Actually, the founders circa 2013 were Patrisse Cullors, Alicia Garza and Opal Tometi, all by their own description "trained Marxists". Sydney University's affiliate foundation awarded them its Sydney Peace Prize a few years back, which should tell you something. Ms Cullors was educated for years by Eric Mann, a member of the domestic terrorist organization Weather Underground. She has named wanted cop-killer Assata Shakur (real name: Joanne Chesimard) as a "leader" who "inspires" her.

I don't know about other States but the sort of Victorians Premier Dan Andrews' indulges to express their views took to the streets *en masse* to love-bomb BLM last June. Unlike pregnant mums in their kitchens and old ladies on park benches, Andrews' personal Praetorian Guard, aka VicPol, made no arrests for violating the state-of-emergency lockdown. (VicPol later issued three organisers with $1652 infringement notices). BLM must indeed be a noble cause if even the coronavirus respects it.

BLM's 37-year-old Ms Cullors has been in the US news lately – but certainly not in the news filtered for us by Their ABC. I see Ms Cullors has been quoted or mentioned in 14 ABC stories from 2017, so the current blackout on ABC news is unusual.

The BLM news coverage in the US has been a bit lively – so much so that Twitter and Facebook felt it their civic duty to shut down any adverse coverage to the best of the unelected tech giants' ability.

The story was broken by the *New York Post* a week ago, the same newspaper that disclosed the lewdly corrupt contents of the laptop owned by Joe Biden's son and randy grifter and crackhead Hunter Biden. Twitter, backed by Facebook, viewed the Hunter Biden story as unfit for consumption by the US electorate, and locked out the *New York Post's* twitter account.

All of the above is my typically long-winded preamble to what Ms Cullors has been up to. While her myrmidons were torching and looting city blocks or smashing statues of George Washington and Abraham Lincoln, Ms Cullors was investing on her personal account in four homes worth at least $US3.2 million. The homes were in exclusive white neighbourhoods, such as Topanga Canyon, just down the road from ritzy Malibu. Topanga has a white population of 88.2 per cent and a black population of 0.4 per cent, according to the 2010 census. She was sniffing around for properties in the Bahamas but the four US homes are the only confirmed investments. She already owned two other homes in Los Angeles.

A celebrity real estate website wrote of her LA investment:

> *A winding 15-minute drive from The Commons at Calabasas and a slightly longer and somewhat less serpentine drive from Malibu's Getty Villa, the pint-sized compound spans about one-quarter of an acre. The property's not-quite 2,400 square feet is divided between the three-bedroom and two-bath main house and a separate one-bed/one-bath apartment capable of hosting guests long term with a private entry and a living room with kitchenette.*

The Post reported Ms Cullors had also been prospecting for Bahamas property at an ultra-exclusive resort where Justin Timberlake and Tiger Woods both have homes. Luxury apartments and townhouses at the beachfront Albany resort, outside Nassau, start at $US5 million and range up to and above $US20 million.

BLM supporters donated $US90m to the international BLM foundation last year alone. Did any of that leak into Ms Cullors' bank accounts? There's no evidence that it did or didn't. Unlike the white policeman she and her mob target, she's entitled to the presumption of innocence. Meanwhile, Michael Brown Sr., the black father of the 18-year-old killed by a Ferguson police officer in 2014, has enjoyed just $US500 from BLM affiliates. Brown Sr. asked: "Why hasn't my family's foundation received any assistance from the movement? How could you leave the families who are helping the community without any funding?" (For some perspective, 511 US cops were feloniously slain on duty in the decade to 2019, including 48 in 2019, plus a luckier 56,034 officers merely assaulted that year).

Accounts filings show that the BLM foundation committed $US21.7 million in grants to official and unofficial BLM chapters and black groups. It ended 2020 with a balance of more than $US60 million, after $US8.4 million expenses.

BLM, whitewashing (or blackwashing) Cullors, said that the criticism "continues a tradition of terror by white supremacists against Black activists" ...

> Patrisse's work for Black people over the years has made her and others who align with the fight for Black liberation targets of racist violence. The narratives being spread about Patrisse have been generated by right-wing forces intent on reducing the support and influence of a movement that is larger than any one organization.
>
> This right-wing offensive not only puts Patrisse, her child and her loved ones in harm's way, it also continues a tradition of terror by white supremacists against Black activists.

Fundraising for Black Lives Matter has been conducted by the left-wing group Thousand Currents, which has a convicted terrorist on its board of directors.

Ms Cullors' personal net worth has risen sharply in line with the global enthusiasm for her cause. Her earnings have arisen from her 2016 book *When They Call You a Terrorist: A Black Lives Matter Memoir*, speaking fees and, last year, a multi-year contract with Warner Bros to produce multi-platform content. The contract value is undisclosed.

It's interesting that she chaired the "Reform LA Jails" group in

2019. The group paid her firm, Janaya & Patrisse Consulting, $US191,000 that year, at the rate of $US20,000 a month. She's the sole owner. Reform LA Jails defended its payments, saying her remuneration was "market rate compensation" for running a $US5 million campaign.

Obviously her concern for LA's jail victims merited some emoluments. However the rate seems a bit high. For example, Claire Rogers, when CEO of World Vision Australia in 2019, was paid $A375,000 ($US290,000) for running a group with revenue of $A583m ($US450m). Reform LA Jails said

> It is hard to comprehend why Black women get scrutinized for being successful and entrepreneurial despite their enormous personal and financial sacrifice and commitment to justice, while white men and others receive accolades for making their millions. It is sexist and racist to expect an executive level Black woman to not be paid for their work.

Twitter is anything but racist, and has demonstrated as much by shutting down whites and blacks alike who disparage Ms Cullors. One critic muzzled by Twitter was black sports journalist Jason Whitlock, who had tweeted sarcastically in her persona, "Black Lives Matter but I don't wanna live around you." He also posted: "Black Lives Matter founder buys $1.4 million home in Topanga, which has a black population of 1.4%. She's with her people!" Twitter said it would unblock him if he deleted his posts, but he replied that he'd stay in "Twitter jail" because he'd done nothing wrong. He added that Ms Cullors in her white neighbourhood "will have plenty of "white cops and white people to complain about."

What's with BLM in general? It's not so nice. The president of Greater New York Black Lives Matter, Hawk Newsome, has warned that "if this country doesn't give us what we want, then we will burn down this system and replace it." The fact of the matter is that more than 90 per cent of black violent deaths – especially of kids and teens — are black-on-black mayhem. White cops kill only about ten unarmed blacks per year (for whatever reasons) whereas polls show US liberals imagine the figure to be 1000-10,000 a year – that's how grotesque the narratives are in the mainstream media. Rather than fret about black-on-black deaths, BLM's website instead focused on how to destroy the nuclear family:

> *We disrupt the Western-prescribed nuclear family structure requirement by supporting each other as extended families and 'villages' that collectively care for one another, especially our children, to the degree that mothers, parents, and children are comfortable.*

Two of the three founders identify as "queer". This might have something to do with the anti-nuclear-family credo.

BLM co-founder Opal Tometi in 2015 tweeted, "Currently in Venezuela. Such a relief to be in a place where there is intelligent political discourse." She wrote of its murderous Marxist dictator Nicolas Maduro:

> *In these last 17 years, we have witnessed the Bolivarian Revolution champion participatory democracy and construct a fair, transparent election system recognized as among the best in the world.*

It pains me to be so negative about BLM. Thousands of BLM enthusiasts in Melbourne and Sydney can't be wrong, can they? #

PART THREE:

THEIR ABC'S "IMPARTIALITY"

The ABC's Slip is Showing

8 August 2020

If the ABC didn't have double standards, it wouldn't have any at all. Case in point: the matter of ABC Adelaide radio host Peter Goers, who has been an ABC radio nightly presenter there for 16 years. He also writes a weekly column in News Corp's *Sunday Mail*, with a prominent tagline below, "Peter Goers can be heard weeknights and Sundays on ABC Radio Adelaide."

In his 26 July 2020 column, this scruffy and overweight Cuba-lover and Israel-hater from the Left wankerati included a prolonged sneer about the (impeccable) dress sense of Liberal MHR Nicolle Flint. His sneers violated the very fibre of the ABC's anti-sexism protocols for respectful treatment of women. But the ABC shrugs off Goers' insults: its Adelaide pet didn't do the sneering on the ABC's own platforms, so move along, nothing to see here.

But, but ... didn't the column tag him as an ABC radio celebrity? Nah, move along, nothing to see here, Nicolle Flint's a Liberal anyway. She's now quitting Parliament, partly because of the Left's harassment.

Here's her back-story. In 2019's federal election her seat of Boothby, with its skinny margin of 2.7%, looked winnable for Labor. An alliance of GetUp, Labor, union muscle and freelance thugs and ferals operated with the full force of its tireless venom. The assault would have given a lesser target a nervous breakdown. The pack saw Flint as everything that the Left and the ABC hates. She's a Peter Dutton and Tony Abbott supporter; she backed the Dutton coup against Prime Minister Turnbull; she won't buy the warmists' catastrophism; and she prefers opportunities to expand workers' and tradies' jobs to underwriting grants for environmentalist piffle artists.

As a 41-year-old single woman living alone, she must have looked vulnerable, and the get-her-to-get-the-seat strategy was good to go. The campaigns were conducted to psychologically damage her, scare her and prevent her freely campaigning, she says.

On her posters, graffiti artists called her a "$60 an hour whore" and "skank" willing to "go and blow". She was shouted down at rallies. Thugs egged and vandalised her office and property of her team was defaced. A stalker with camera was so persistent and upsetting that she called in the police, who gave the creep an anti-stalk warning. She remained fearful that her home address would become known and a target.

Mass phone-outs by GetUp volunteers included calls describing her as 'evil' and seeking to tear her down personally via verballing with loaded language. (GetUp denies even an iota of uncouthness).

At the height of the campaign, the ABC reporters tried gaslighting her with lines like: "Liberal MP Nicolle Flint has refused to answer questions about whether she regrets supporting the call for a leadership spill that ousted former prime minister Malcolm Turnbull." (The ABC's shills couldn't imagine Turnbull's ouster as anything but an electoral disaster for the Liberals). Not to miss an opportunity, the national broadcaster put itself at GetUp's service with lead paragraphs like this: "Activist group GetUp has named South Australian MP Nicolle Flint the state's 'most backwards politician' and has launched a push to unseat her from the electorate of Boothby."

With such daily pressure over the course of five-or-so months, it was surprising she made it through. What she endured also stands as a horror-story warning for any and every conservative woman considering a career in politics.

In the event, the "progressives" and their tactics alienated Boothby voters and much of the Adelaide public. Flint held the seat narrowly, but with a 3.5 per cent increase in her personal vote.

For the Left and its ABC spear-carriers, the pile-on must never cease while she holds Boothby. Hence Peter Goers' column last week mocking her and the way she dresses. His ostensible justification was MPs' alleged over-use of taxpayer funding to showcase their wares: the allowance is a staple of political life. To amplify his faux indignation, he reminded his readers of Ms Flint's sympathies for Abbott and climate non-conformity. I'll furnish the details shortly, but let's skip now to Ms Flint's astonishing response.

She has tweeted a one-minute home-made video re-capping Goers' "sexist rubbish" and asks, "So Mr Goers, what should a woman in politics wear? How about a garbage bag to match your rubbish views?"

She takes off her black coat to show herself wearing a grey bin-bag tied with a black belt. As a political stunt, even some female Labor MPs said they loved it.

The plot thickened when the ABC's political writer Jane Norman felt compelled to cover — or, rather, spin — the story about her ABC colleague's discomfiture. The spin involved her re-capping mild sexisms by Liberal politicians and supporters, the technique known as "Look over there, a squirrel!" She included, of course, pundit Alan Jones' hyperbole that Julia Gillard should be put in a "chaff bag" and dumped at sea and Tony Abbott saying (2013) his fellow-candidate Fiona Scott had "sex appeal". She didn't have space to include Tony Abbott's looking at his watch while Prime Minister Julia Gillard hectored him. Ms Norman ended her report with a mysterious circumlocution: "Mr Goers has been contacted for comment." Perhaps the ABC's Goers told the ABC's Norman to get lost, or he went into hiding from her. The trail then runs cold; nothing more is published that I can find from the ABC on the ABC's rogue or disappearing Mail columnist.

Goers in 2013, like the profane one-time ABC employee Mike Carlton in 2020, scored an OAM "for service to the community." ABC Local Content Manager in South Australia Graeme Bennett, congratulating Goers, said at the time, "Peter's contribution to

PART III

ABC Local Radio has been immense, but his contribution to our community has been greater still. Since he joined 891 ABC Adelaide in 2004, he has shown his true colours: compassion, humour and a love of his home state and every person in it. We're absolutely thrilled at this humbling honour, and privileged to work with a great South Australian. Onya Goersy."

You probably want to know, what exactly did "Goersy" write about the female MHR? Answer:

> *In her latest glossy, six-page brochure there are 23 photos of Nicolle. There's Nicolle with troubled MP Sam Duluk, Nicolle with constituents, Nicolle with ministers, a curious photo of a photographer taking her photo, and Nicolle with a photo of an over-dressed old lady – oh, it's the Queen.*
>
> *There's lots about what Nicolle has been up to but no mention of her support for Peter Dutton, Tony Abbot, bank CEOs and climate change sceptics.*
>
> *Nicolle wears pearl earrings and a pearly smile. She favours a vast wardrobe of blazers, coats and tight, black, ankle-freezing trousers and stiletto heels. She's presents herself in her own newsletter, 23 times as a fashion plate. She has blazers and coats in black, blue, pink, red, beige, green, white, cream, floral and two in grey ...*

(The ABC itself, by the way, has a thing for stiletto heels. Like every Melbournian, I'm bombarded evenings with that ABC promo about Leftist Virginia Trioli strutting Southbank in her stilettos, to the Nancy Sinatra song that ends, "One of these days these boots are gunna walk all over you").

So this week Quadrant Online queried ABC management. The exchange went:

> On July 26 Sunday Mail published a comment piece by the ABC's Peter Goers, with his ABC status well displayed at the bottom of the piece: 'Peter Goers can be heard weeknights and Sundays on ABC Radio Adelaide'.
>
> The piece (in my view) was a gratuitously sexist attack on a female elected politician, Nicolle Flint, in violation of numerous ABC guidelines to staff against sexist reporting. I have also studied the guidelines on "Comment" pieces and consider it violates them as well.
>
> The ABC published a news story mentioning (mid-way) Goers' comments and Flint's 'garbage bag' response, but this news story failed to deal with or mention the failure of Goer to observe ABC guidelines.
>
> It also said, "Mr Goers has been contacted for comment." It seems one ABC staffer, Peter Goers, is unable or unwilling to respond publicly to another, Jane Norman.
>
> My questions are:
>
> 1/ Is Goers a full-time staff member of ABC? If not, what is his ABC status?
>
> 2/ What reaction or response, if any, has ABC management made publicly in relation to the sexism in the comment piece by its employee Goers? Ditto, what response internally?

PART III

3/ Did Goers ever respond to the request for comment by your reporter Jane Norman?

4/ If so, where do I find that response? If not, given that ABC is an advocate for fully informed reporting, will management compel Goers to respond publicly?

5/ Is it consistent with ABC guidelines for Goers to refer to Queen Elizabeth 11 as "an overdressed old lady?"

6/ Has Goers apologised publicly in any way for his sexist comments?

7/ Is there a double standard at the ABC that sexist attacks on conservative politicians and the Queen are not as serious as equivalent attacks on, say, Penny Wong or Julia Gillard?

With commendable speed, I received a reply within hours from ABC media PR John Woodward, herewith:

> Peter Goers' remarks regarding the appearance of politicians, was published in his regular Adelaide Sunday Mail column under the heading "Bin the pollies' newsletters along with corflutes" (Sunday Mail, Sunday 26 July, 2020).
>
> As his comments were published in The Sunday Mail, your questions regarding the appropriateness of those remarks should be directed to the publishers, News Corp, and not to the ABC.
>
> As well as being a weekly columnist for The Sunday Mail, Peter Goers also presents the Evenings program on ABC Radio Adelaide. He has not repeated his views expressed in his 26th July Sunday Mail column on ABC Radio. Our guidelines cover what is broadcast on our airwaves and/or published on our digital and social media

platforms and therefore are not relevant to this issue.

Requests for comment by Peter Goers received by the ABC on this issue were referred to The Sunday Mail for a response. We are unaware if The Sunday Mail and/or Peter Goers responded to those requests. Again, you will need to follow up that line of enquiry with The Sunday Mail.

This response suggests there's been a major change of policy by the ABC. It seems that ABC presenters and reporters can now say, write or publish whatever inflammatory or hate speech (against the Right) that they like, whether politically partisan, sexist, racist, non-inclusive or gratuitously offensive to the vulnerable, providing they do not present these views on the ABC or its various sub-platforms.

The ABC has formal guidelines for staff, saying that their on-ABC and off-ABC behaviour should not bring the ABC into disrepute or reflect on its impartiality. But in this case, despite Goers touting his ABC credentials on his hit-piece against Ms Flint, ABC spokesman John Woodward says Goers' Sunday Mail scribblings are nothing to do with the ABC, and I should take my complaints to the Sunday Mail itself. Indeed, says Mr Woodward, "Our guidelines cover what is broadcast on our airwaves and/or published on our digital and social media platforms and therefore are not relevant to this issue."

I don't think so, Mr Woodward. Try this:

External work and Editorial Conflicts

PART III

> *1.4 External activities of individuals undertaking work for the ABC must not undermine the independence and integrity of the ABC's editorial content...* (Would Goers' love affair with Cuba undermine the ABC's integrity a bit?)

> *4.3 Do not state or imply that any perspective is the editorial opinion of the ABC.* (Doesn't the Sunday Mail tagline about Goers' ABC job also suggest something about ABC narratives?)

Another set of ABC guidelines for staff, INDEPENDENCE, INTEGRITY AND RESPONSIBILITY says,

> *The trust and respect of the community depend on the ABC's editorial independence and integrity. Independence and responsibility are inseparable ... It is fundamentally important that the ABC's content is not improperly influenced by political, sectional, commercial or personal interests.*

Would any of Australia's Coalition voters — roughly 50% at any recent election — trust Goers or the ABC after reading his columns?

Moreover, the ABC editorial Style Guide warns,

> *Don't make gratuitous references to a woman's physical appearance if you wouldn't do the same for a man.*

The ABC Board is well-stocked with ardent feminists. I'd love to know these ladies' views about an ABC staffer trash-talking in the *Sunday Mail* about a much put-upon female elected to Parliament by the ABC's public.

179

What to make of all this? First, Don't believe Goers. Second: Don't trust the ABC. And third, when it comes to crusading against sexism, there are no greater hypocrites than the Left's gender warriors.

As Herald Sun/Sky News commentator Rita Panahi puts it, Leftists "preach women's rights but then they attack any woman who challenges their warped view of the world."

End-note: On 27 February 2021 Nicolle Flint announced she would not re-contest her seat of Boothby and would exit politics. Colleagues attributed her decision to the sustained bullying and harassment by her Labor, GetUp and Extinction Rebellion opponents. #

PART III

It's official: ABC porn for kids is fine

13 October 2020; 6 November 2020; 24 January 2021 and 7 February 2021.

The ABC aims to provide children and young people (under the age of 18) with enjoyable and enriching content, as well as opportunities for them to express themselves. ABC Annual Report, 2019-20, p185.

I'd better apologise to the ABC. I've been carrying on about ABCTV broadcasting pornography to 15-year-old schoolchildren, when all along the ABC was operating perfectly within its rights and codes, according to the Commonwealth Ombudsman.

The Ombudsman now endorses the same view I got from the Australian Communications and Media Authority. ABCTV doesn't even need to self-rate its pornography at the most severe MA15+ level. An ordinary M rating is quite OK for ABCTV animated graphics about triple-penetrating a woman, defecating during coitus in a hotel corridor, raping a woman from behind with a two-metre penis, and a male buggering a dog. All that and more was presented as entertainment in just one of the nine episodes of "comedy" series At *Home Alone Together.*

Episode 9 included "jokes" about a crowded household moving into a woman's vagina, where there would be more room. But the Ombudsman says it's fine and dandy that the ABC gives it the same "M" — "Adult Themes, Violence" — as the BBC's ever-so-mild *Midsomer Murders.*

The *Home Alone* series aired at 9pm Wednesdays from May 13. The commercial channels would run a mile from broadcasting filth, not just from moral scruples but because filth would be poison to advertisers. Case in point: in 1992 Channel 9 ran a show, *Australia's naughtiest home videos*. It included a man with his head wedged between a dancer's breasts, animal genitalia and animal sex, a man lifting a barbell with his penis and footage of a couple having outdoor sex. The network's owner, Kerry Packer, was watching the show at home. He lifted the phone and ordered: "Get that shit off the air!" The production team hastily complied, lying to viewers about "a technical problem". They filled in the rest of the hour with a repeat of a serial.

In contrast, ABC chair Ita Buttrose and her executives, far from phoning in to say, "Get that *Home Alone* shit off the air!" cited it as "morale-boosting" in the ABC's 2019-20 annual report:

> Other morale-boosting new programs included *At Home Alone Together*, a comedic take on the lifestyle magazine genre that went from concept to screen in just six weeks.

The "ever genial" creator of the series Nick Hayden was promoted a month or two later to become head of the ABC's entire entertainment empire. He replaced Josie Mason-Campbell, who had exited in the course of a budget-led restructure in June. She cited *Home Alone* as part of her entertainment track record, saying, "I have been privileged to work with the ABC and to lead a ridiculously talented and creatively brave factual and entertainment team."

PART III

I have now completed a trifecta of failed complaints about the ABCTV pornography for kids. Here's the chronology.

The ABC's supposedly independent complaints panel on 5 November 2020 threw out my complaint without considering it. It relied on an ABC technicality that complaints later than six weeks after broadcast date are "out of time". In fact I'd accessed the material from iview, where it remains accessible to schoolchildren under and over 15 to this day and at all hours of the day. The six-week technicality relates to some pre-digital practice of ABCTV dumping tapes of inconsequential material after six weeks to reduce clutter in their cupboards.

I appealed to the Australian Communications and Media Authority (ACMA) against the ABC. ACMA on 22 January, 2021 informed me that it had "carefully assessed" my complaint, and reviewed the material on iview. In an implicit rebuke to the ABC, it ignored the "six week out of time" technicality. But ACMA still ruled that, in context, the "M" ratings were fine. "Consequently, it [the material] is unlikely to constitute a breach of the ABC's Code and as a result, we will not be taking further action."

I appealed to the Commonwealth Ombudsman on 27 January 2021, saying, "I would like ACMA to revisit my appeal against ABC Complaints Panel and issue a public statement that the ABC wrongly classified its pornographic materials as M. I would like you to direct ABCTV to broadcast no further pornography to schoolchildren, regardless of whether ABCTV views its pornography as 'comedy'."

With blinding and commendable speed, I had a nearly-900-word response from an Ombudsman staffer named Mark within 24 hours. Perhaps the office had nothing else on its plate that day and the whole organisation focused on my email. So why have I delayed reporting the reply? It's because, at the foot of the Ombudsman's email, there was a dire warning that unauthorised publication of the contents could incur "legal sanctions". So I wrote back to Mark and asked for permission to publish. Again with commendable speed, I received back a friendly email saying, "I apologise for the delay in responding to your query. While I can't offer you a legal opinion on the question you have raised, I don't believe there would be an issue with circulating our response given that the response only includes references to material you have provided to our Office and material that is already in the public domain."

I can say sincerely that the Ombudsman's office is a credit to the federal public service, both in courtesy and efficiency. As for appealing against the ruling, I've got nowhere to go now but the Federal or High Courts. Where's the Privy Council when you need it?

By now you might be wondering if I've made everything up and I'm just pulling your leg. Nope. Every word is true and verifiable. I'd better give you the full story. First, I'll background how the ABC brought At *Home Alone* into existence. Second, I'll spell out just how far into pornography the creators went. Third, I'll measure *Home Alone* against the ABC's perpetual clamour for greater respect for women and for protection of children. Finally I'll document my failed crusade against *At Home Alone*.

The background

The ABC in early 2020 blurbed that *At Home* collected "Australia's best comedians and revered actors to give audiences advice on how they can live their best life in the time of COVID-19." It would be "an extraordinary project for this unprecedented time," according to the ABC's then Head of Entertainment and Factual, Josie Mason-Campbell.

The goal was to use its taxpayer funds to further bail out the unemployed community of leftist arty types. The extent of this largesse has not been disclosed nor ever will be, if the ABC has any say in the matter.

Online Investment Manager at Screen Australia, Lee Naimo, said the show "will entertain a nation hungry for relevant content while employing a sector of the industry hungry to flex their comedy muscles. I can't wait to see what these teams bring together in these unique circumstances." Said Screen Australia, "So, Australia, come and meet your new best friends who are here to help you through the crisis!"

These "new best friends" were the ABC's usual luvvie suspects, presented by "beloved national treasure" Ray Martin, in the ABC's tradition of paying its superannuated once-weres like Kerry

O'Brien and Barry Cassidy new bucket-loads of money to clamber back on our screens. Other lefty celebs with walk-on parts included Leigh Sales, Sydney red-bandanna-man Peter FitzSimons, the ABC's sometimes-correct medico Dr Norman Swan, plus elderly ex-priest and friend to the Occupy movement Father Bob Maguire.

The sheltered-workshop nature of the series is suggested by its vast roll-call of staff: 13 directors, 11 producers and nearly 50 writers.

Senior producers included several of the team that made the low-rated and dumped *Tonightly* show. In one *Tonightly* episode in March 2018, comedian/presenter Greg Larsen called Australian Conservative candidate Kevin Bailey a c**t. In the four-minute *Tonightly* rant, which was pre-approved by ABC executives for broadcast, there were eight "c**s" and two "f**s".

What the ABC called the "explosively funny" *Home Alone* series was supposed to comprise sketches about do-it-yourself projects, wellness, kid-wrangling, and personal finances but was hijacked by creators fixated on large penises, single and two-sex fellatio and coprophilia, which you might know is "abnormal interest and pleasure in faeces and defecation."

One of *Home Alone's* brought-in actresses was banned from Twitter in 2018 for posts: "Oi Scott Morrison, I'm gonna chop your f***king head off … Every politician is a disgusting c—t. I honestly think we need to chop their heads off."

Home Alone's distasteful contents

The *Home Alone* tone is set from three minutes into Episode 1 by a Harry Potter take-off: "Why don't you show me that big hard wand … why don't you spank me with that." It degenerates to actress Becky Lucas in role saying, "Maybe it's another wizard girl from another house and she wants to suck your dick or lick my … I would love to give Dobbie a little gobbie … I would love to be moaning like Myrtle."

In Episode 2 in a woman's erotic fiction fantasy a male character opens his pants to expose his large penis, and the female says, "All right let's have a look. My, my we have been working out! You can't beat the real thing, welcome to cougar town." Then she kneels to fellate him.

Episode 4 features the most enhanced pornography. It's a challenge to allocate responsibility for this episode, rather like discovering who decided to hire Victoria's private hotel quarantine guards rather than police enforcers. The episode lists two executive producers, one Series producer, five producer/directors, and one contributing director, plus a "Screen Australia production executive". It is striking that Episode 4 had its own ABC "Editorial Policy Adviser", one Simon Melkman.

In the episode's "Important Message for Footballers" a woman in voice-over says *Home Alone* has "introduced a bonk ban to keep players safe." At 12mins 50secs, a graphic about "triple penetration" shows a stylised naked woman crouched on all fours, straddling a naked man who reaches up to grasp her torso. The prone man is penetrating her vaginally. Behind the crouching woman, another naked man kneels, penetrating her anally while grasping her hips. The "triple" element involves a standing man grasping her head to push her mouth onto his penis.

The segment continues, "'A cup of tea is fine, vaginal contact is out.' A full-screen graphic shows two simplified human figures having sex in missionary position. 'Discussing literature is all good, vigorous rogering is bad.' (The animated man enters a woman from behind while she leans against a table.) 'So does that mean I can't behave like a footballer anymore?' No, urinating in public is still fine (man urinates against a lamp post) but sex is out (woman rides man in reverse cowgirl position). Taking a dump in a hotel is fine (man defecates in a hotel corridor). Just don't have sex while you take the dump. (Man defecates while entering a woman from behind).

Simulating sex with a dog (a standing man holds a dog waist-high), that was never really fine. 'But can I still bonk if my penis is 2 metres long and I socially distance throughout the bonk?' (Man with 2m penis enters a woman from behind while she leans against a table). While we are all extremely impressed, no, that is not allowed. Come on, be a sport. Australia needs its footie back so please don't have a sex life, so the rest of us can have a life."

Some of the schematised human graphic and animated figures can also be viewed (I'm told) on the world-prominent porn site redtube.com. At first I thought that the ABCTV producers had acquired them from redtube.com, but this is improbable as animated graphics like the 2 metre penis must have been tailor-made for the series' Covid context. The design work was perhaps assisted by the two people named in the credits closing the episode as "motion graphics" specialists.

Episode 8 features the "glory hole" in public toilets where one man can fellate another anonymously through a hole in a wall. I didn't know about "glory holes" until 2016 when I was checking some green-gay performance art for my Quadrant article *Sex Pistils at the Oz Council Bathhouse*. The ABC "joke" substitutes handshakes through a larger wall-hole, in lieu of fellatio. The "comedy" writers also do a mock Four Corners exposing "the shady corporate underbelly" about frustrated business men unable to shake hands. Instead they visit the hole at a "disgusting public toilet" or "shake spot". The hole is also large enough for banknote payments to be first passed through. Dialogue: "It's 50 bucks for a handshake, or 70 for a nice firm one." "What about a wet one?"

Next scene, "depraved members of amateur sporting teams" – the ABC seems to have special animus against footballers – line up at multiple holes for "consecutive shakes". It took me a while to get the double entendre on "shakes" and wish I hadn't.

You're probably wondering why Episode 7 alone got that "MA" rating. It's actually not the worst for crassness. It has a character "Mary Seymour" bragging about her "multiple lovers", and she thanks one elderly lover for "bringing me to arousal in the shower this morning". She tries to get a romance going for a very old lady by giving her conversation cards reading, "What is your favourite blow-job technique?", "Who gave you your first orgasm?" and "Are you good in bed?"

Episode 5 is particularly gross. "Mary Seymour", 60, says: "People think things start slowing down in the bedroom but I have never been more sexually active. I love penises of all shapes and sizes (illustrated with half a dozen eclairs. She licks cream from one of them). Why have one when you can have many, I have multiple lovers and talk about them in my cabaret show, The Sixty Year Old Slut." It continues:

> Young man to Mary: *I love to curl up in your arms and read a book.*
>
> Mary: *Well I like to see your dick and while working towards arousal get my big breasts out. Maybe I should get into my maid's uniform.*
>
> Older man: *Fuck yeah.*

It's a rare episode of *Home Alone* that doesn't have half a dozen big-penis jokes. In Episode 4, for example, bogan Nate says, "Stealing is fine — morals are only for rich people. Well that was a success. I nearly got pinched for the salami (pulls a huge salami out of pants) but I just told them that I had a really big dong." He wobbles the foot-long salami like an erect penis. A placard says, "Nate says: Pretend salami is your dick."

In Episode 5, TV gardener Costa Georgiadis is naked but with pixelated privates. He prunes his pubic hair with a brush-cutter.

PART III

The sketch cuts to Ray Martin fingering Christmas decorations and saying, "Nice balls."

In Episode 8, Ray Martin pretends to audition as another character, Jason, saying, "Hey I'm Jason, you wanna see my (bleeping) dick?"

In Episode 7, character "Mary Seymour" says, "I think girls of all ages should have a nice big juicy bum. One (lover) had a penis of normal size and the other penis was pretty small."

Episode 6 could be sub-titled 'Defecation City'. At 2.50 minutes in we get a "parenting tip" from an actor sitting on the toilet: "Doing a poo is a great way to talk shit on-line." Six minutes later, and actress Becky Lucas in character is discussing with her beau why a fly landed on her. "What are flies attracted to?" and they both reply, "Like shit, turd, poop, poo." Beau says, "Maybe I have equated you with that in my head now. You are shit so I'm moving on."

A couple of minutes later there's a sketch of an adult sister saying to her adult brother, "You make me feel like I want to take a shit on your head." Their emotion chart reads "Pooping, Horny, Anger, Sadness." Episode 8 ends with a placard, "F*ck that's yum as sh*t."

In *Home Alone*, Christianity is much mocked, as you would expect, with the cooperation of elderly real-life Father Bob Maguire (RC). Zingers he delivers include mock confessionals like

> # Hail Marys for everyone, what you saw in the confessional stays in

the confessional except for the bits I use. You can shut down our life but you can't shut down salvation. (Episode 2)

\# *Absolution for all, because they can shut down our lives but they can't shut down our afterlife.* (Episode 3)

The ABC "comedians" don't mock Islam. The Charlie Hebdo massacre in Paris was probably a disincentive.

It hardly needs saying that the *Home Alone* "comedy" writers pile up the Green-Left propaganda: this is, after all, their ABC. Episode 8 has a peculiar segment where Ray Martin jokingly claims he's been personally spreading the virus to VIPs. He shows a pic of Vice-President Pence and Prince Charles and says he's "often having a good sniff of their hair before infecting them from a vial." As those getting their news from the ABC would not know, Joe Biden, now President, is notorious for sniffing the hair of women and small girls, while doing and saying creepy things to girls around puberty. Martin's line about "having a good sniff of their hair" must have originated from Biden's fetishes but the "comedy" writers got cold feet and deleted any Biden reference. That leaves Martin's "good sniff" remark hanging in mid-air.

This being Their ABC, its "comedians" also whine about their ABC having only $1 billion every year to bless itself with.

\# "Enjoy ABC Kids before it's defunded!"

\# Ray Martin: "That's it for a week. Sadly due to ABC budget cuts that's the end of the Auslan [sign language] services as well."

Placard: "Ray Martin, sadly surviving the ABC cuts."

These artists will typically plead to conservative ministers for funds and then use those funds to excoriate the government in vilest terms.

Sex aside, Episode 7 has the best line of the show. Garden guru Costa Georgiadis says to Ray Martin: "This celery is just like your show. It's limp, there's nothing new about it. It leaves a nasty stale taste in your mouth."

ABC's hypocritical concern for women and children

There's nothing more sanctimonious than the ABC's annual reports.

> *The ABC acknowledges that a public broadcaster should never gratuitously harm or offend and accordingly any content which is likely to harm or offend must have a clear editorial purpose … Avoid the unjustified use of stereotypes or discriminatory content that could reasonably be interpreted as condoning or encouraging prejudice* (2020 report, p184).

Want more?

> *Classification has progressively exhibited heightened sensibilities with respect to editorial concerns in children's programming … There is far greater oversight of children's programming …*

The ABC's normal chatter is that boys are influenced by males' endemic disparagement of women. This leads to boys, young men and adult males' contempt for females, in turn generating males' domestic violence and sexual assault. In 2016 the ABC was barraging viewers with government anti-domestic-violence ads showing boys slamming doors on girls and chauvinist fathers telling boys "Don't throw like a girl, mate!" The ad's voice-over says, "Violence against women starts with disrespect. The excuses we make allow it to grow. Violence against women: let's stop it at the start." Well said but …

Home Alone's misogyny screened just a couple of months after the ABC's International Women's Day extravaganza featuring a cringe-worthy "all-female line-up across capital city Local Radio, ABC Classic and RN, as well as 24 hours of songs, stories, and discussions from female artists and presenters on triple j, Double J and triple j Unearthed." (p67).

We discover ABC board members' feminist credentials on opening pages of the report. Ita Buttrose is a founding member and former president of Chief Executive Women. Trump-hating deputy chair Kirstin Ferguson has been a board member of SheStarts, and Chair of the Women's Agenda Leadership Awards. She's a member of Chief Executive Women, Women Corporate Directors and the Women's Leadership Institute of Australia. Donny Walford is a Founding Member of International Women's Forum Australia, and a former director of Australian Women's Chamber of Commerce and Industry. Georgie Somerset's past roles include with the National Foundation for Australian Women.

The ABC role-plays as champion for women, with its more than

53 per cent female staff and 51 per cent female executives. Target for ABC news stories is for 50-50 representation of women and "a commitment to content that is relevant to women." I guess the *Home Alone* schematic of a woman being entered from behind by a two-metre penis would be included as female-relevant content.

The ABC is battling the federal government to retain self-rating of its programs, rather than ratings by independent third parties. In submissions, the ABC prated:

> *The [ABC] Corporation maintains a rigorous Editorial Policies framework to ensure that high standards are met and the ABC is accountable to audiences through the co-regulatory regime with the ACMA [Australian Communications and Media Authority]. The ABC Editorial Policies state that the Corporation's broadcast and publication of comprehensive and innovative content requires a willingness to take risks, invent and experiment with new ideas, while taking care not to gratuitously cause harm or offence ...*
>
> *The Corporation recognises that it has a privileged place in the media landscape, with access to spectrum and public funding ...*
>
> *The ABC believes any dilution of its independence, however subtle, may have a chilling effect on its ability to fulfil its core functions, including delivering diverse, innovative and sometimes controversial content to audiences.*
>
> *ABC audiences can understand precisely what to expect at each classification level and can rest assured that the decisions made by ABC classifiers have been made as objectively as possible. The existing approach is effective, audience centred, responsible and responsive."* [As if.]

Official responses to my complaints

Here's what I got from the ABC's supposedly independent complaints panel, 4 November, 2020:

> *Audience and Consumer Affairs will generally not accept for investigation complaints lodged more than six weeks after an item was broadcast or published. As you have not indicated that any special circumstances apply in this instance, we decline to investigate your complaint. Yours sincerely, Lauren Crozier, ABC Audience & Consumer Affairs.*

In fact my complaint did note special circumstances: "My complaint is probably past six weeks of the screenings but I have accessed the programs – as many 15-year-olds would, through iview. I trust the six week test will not be used to invalidate my complaint."

On 22 January 2021, I got this response to my appeal against the ABC to the Australian Broadcasting and Communications Authority. (Emphases added).

> *We appreciate your patience while we gave due consideration to the issues raised in your complaint. We understand you were concerned that seven of the At Home Alone Together episodes included sexual references and depictions that exceeded the program's classification. In particular you were concerned that this would endanger the welfare of schoolchildren aged 15 years and over.*
>
> *We have carefully assessed your complaint, including reviewing copies of the broadcasts and considered the relevant provisions from the Code. The relevant broadcasts were classified M, with*

consumer advice that variously included 'adult themes', 'sexual references' and 'coarse language'. The ABC's Associated Standard on Television Program Classification states that, at the M level, most themes can be dealt with, **but the treatment should be discreet and the impact should not be strong, sexual activity may be discreetly implied**, and coarse language may be used.

The content of concern largely consisted of verbal sexual references and innuendo. We also carefully assessed the 'bonk ban' sketch that you described in detail from episode four and noted it was a series of animated graphics of sexual acts undertaken by stick figures **(akin to the pictograms typically used on toilet doors to denote figures of different sex)**. It did not contain any nudity or implied, simulated or actual sexual acts **by real people.** [Describing the animated persons engaged in sex acts as "stick figures" is sophistry].

In program classification, verbal sexual references are generally considered to be less impactful than visual depictions. Graphical or animated representations would also have correspondingly less impact **than depictions of real people performing or simulating sexual acts.** [More sophistry. Check out the pornographic cartoon industry or Japanese "manga" comics]. Impact, and therefore classification, is also influenced by the amount of visual detail.

In summary, we have conducted a detailed assessment of your complaint. While we appreciate that the matter was of concern to you, and taking the above matters into account, including the program context, we consider that, while the 'bonk ban' sketch was **more impactful** than other material you had cited in your complaint, the material we reviewed **was unlikely to exceed the M classification.** Consequently, **it is unlikely to constitute a breach of the ABC's Cod**e and as a result, **we will not be taking further action.** Yours sincerely, Paul Kernebone, A/g Manager, Content Investigations Section.

I appealed against ACMA to the Commonwealth Ombudsman and on 28 January 2021 I received this response from staffer "Mark". Emphases added:

OFFICIAL

I have considered your complaint, but have decided **not to investigate.** *My view is that ACMA's decision was* **not unreasonable** *and I cannot see a good basis to conclude that investigating the complaint would result in ACMA changing the decision.*

I understand you strongly disagree with ACMA's decision that a number of broadcasts of the sketch show "At Home Alone Together" did not appear likely to have breached relevant sections of the ABC Code of Practice 2019. [It would be good for Staffer Mark to use fewer double negatives.]

In your complaint you suggested that ACMA's decision was "capricious, arbitrary and wrong". [Correction: I said the ABC Complaints Panel, not ACMA, had been capricious, arbitrary and wrong]. **I cannot see a basis for concluding the decision was either capricious or arbitrary.** *It seems clear that ACMA* *considered the issues you raised, viewed the program, and assessed it against the Code. As to whether the decision was wrong, my assessment is that there was* **a not unreasonable basis for ACMA's decision.**

In my experience in assessing complaints about ACMA, whether the complaint involves the ABC or a commercial broadcaster, it is often the case that viewers or listeners find that the relevant code **doesn't provide the kind of protections or restrictions that they may expect.** *Standard 7 of the ABC Code provides an illustrative example of this in that it* **does not actively prevent** *the broadcast of content that is* **likely to harm or offend.** *Instead, the Standard merely requires that such content has a clear purpose, is prefaced by clear warnings when applicable, and takes into account community standards – noting that the Australian community is diverse, which means that* **what is acceptable content will depends [sic] on the particular context,** *including the nature of the content and its target audience.*

You will note that Standard 7.1 requires that one take into account the editorial context in which the content is broadcast, while Standard 7.2 **allows for content likely to cause harm or offence to be broadcast** *if it is accompanied by proper warning labels, advice, and/or classification labels.*

On viewing the program, it is clear that it is a comedic program that aims to amuse by satirising a standard lifestyle program. While I accept that many viewers may not have found the material amusing, it is clear that satire is the context in which to consider the program.

This necessarily means one would expect to find content employing exaggeration, ridicule, absurdity, and inappropriate or unusual behaviour. [Really? Such as raping a dog?] *Importantly, understanding this was not left entirely up to the viewer as the broadcasts were also prefaced by advice such as 'adult themes', 'sexual references' and 'coarse language'* [Such as a lady saying, "suck your dick or lick my ..."].

I acknowledge your view that the content wasn't appropriate for an M classification, **but I don't see a good basis to conclude that ACMA's assessment was wrong.** *Under the ABC's Associated Standard on Television Program Classification, a program classified as M is recommended for people aged 15 years and over. While there is an expectation that* **"less explicit or less intense material will be included in the M classification", explicit material may be broadcast under the M classification,** *including content that "is considered to be potentially harmful or disturbing to those under 15 years". This means that depending on the particular content, a satirical program such as At Home Alone Together* **does not require an MA classification.**

The primary content ACMA focused on in assessing whether the broadcasts breached Standard 7.3 was the so-called 'bonk ban' sketch. This was because of an assessment that this material was likely to be more impactful than other material you cited. In essence ACMA found that the offending animations in that sketch were **so lacking in detail and were shown for such a short period** *that, when seen in the context of a satirical program that was prefaced with warnings about* *sexual references, the sketch* **did not clearly exceed the M classification.** *In my view ACMA's assessment of this material* **was not unreasonable.**

As I do not see a basis on which we could be critical of ACMA's assessment in this case nor have reason to believe that an investigation would result in a different substantive outcome, I have decided that **an investigation of your complaint is not warranted.**

I appreciate that you may be disappointed in this decision [I am]. Should you wish to discuss this decision, please contact me by reply email.

Yours sincerely, Mark, Complaint Resolution Officer

COMMONWEALTH OMBUDSMAN

Influencing systemic improvement in public administration

The Office of the Commonwealth Ombudsman acknowledges the traditional owners of country throughout Australia and their continuing connection to land, culture and community. We pay our respects to elders past and present.

To sum up, the ABC Code (Standards 7.1-7.3) offers the public no protection against ABCTV's broadcasting of pornography, except that such material should be in an "editorial context", properly self-rated by ABCTV as M or MA15+, meet standards of some element of the community (bikie gangs, perhaps?), and include a warning about sexual themes, strong language, violence etc.

Strictures about such programs screening after 8.30pm are

worthless given that they remain accessible by children of any age at any time on iview.

The only bulwarks against pornography being broadcast on ABCTV are the hoped-for decency, good taste and professionalism of ABC management. In the case of *At Home Alone Together*, ABC management was au contraire delighted by the material.

It is a fair point that the nine-part *Home Alone* series contains a lot of harmless (but lame) humour. The pornography and filth are extras. A few items on *At Home Alone* are genuinely funny, although possibly inadvertent, like the ABC person "coming out" as heterosexual in Episode 9. It's great for the ABC to be so inclusive. *[I self-rate this joke as "satire" or "comedy", classification MA15+, strong language warning and any harm or offence is justified by editorial context and modern community standards]*.

That ABCTV material was all 2020. In February 2021 ABCTV broadcast new "comedy": *Why are you like this? Episode 3: D-ck or P-ssy of Color. After another bad date with a white guy, Mia decolonises her p-ssy*. Rated M (not MA+). Hmm. Should I complain again? #

PART III

Some Riots, the Left Kind, Don't Distress the ABC at all

12 January 2021

What a mystery! Pundit Laura Tingle on ABCTV's 7.30 last night (January 11) showed 13 seconds of clippage from 1996 of a crowd surging towards Parliament House in Canberra. We got glimpses of blokes pushing and shoving at the doors and at police lines, and then half a dozen police and blokes wrestling inside the foyer. She explained, after bagging President Trump for allegedly inciting the Capitol Hill riots, "It is not as if Australia has not witnessed its own physical attacks on its Parliament." Cut to 1996 ACTU secretary Bill Kelty saying, "If they [L-NCP] want to fight, if they want a war, we will have a full set."

Tingle says that Kelty "rightly" feared a new Howard government would represent "an assault on union power". The union anti-Howard campaign led to a rally at Parliament House "that turned ugly". After our 13-second glimpse of the ugliness, Tingle lined up Howard plus Opposition Leader Kim Beazley later condemning the violence – although Beazley in fact had revved up the crowd at the time. With concerned frowns to suggest ABC gravitas, Tingle wrapped up her historical excursion thus: "But there is a difference between an assault from outside the system [What? The ACTU and the federal Opposition are outside the Australian system?] and one encouraged by the man [Trump] at its very heart."

They say history doesn't necessarily repeat, but it does rhyme. And what a close rhyme there is between that mob invading Parliament

House, Canberra on August 19, 1996, and the mob of mainly Trump supporters that broke into the Capitol last week.

Both incursions were indefensible: violent behaviour is bad, and worse when directed at any nation's legislative chamber. Of the thousands of Australian "progressives" who stormed and looted our Parliament on that August 19, 1996, fewer than dozen were charged. I'm hanged if I can find out if any were convicted or fined, let alone jailed. On the other hand, I hope, like Craig Kelly, that all American demonstrators who committed offences in or around the Capitol get their legal desserts, and especially the Antifa thugs who ran false-flag operations there.

The Australian rioters and looters at Parliament were part of a national "cavalcade" to Canberra of some 25,000 unionists and supporters organised by the Australian Council of Trade Unions and backed by the Opposition, students peeved about their shrinking government stipends, Aboriginals by the hundreds peeved about reductions to their ATSIC money, rent-a-ferals and drunken agitators.

Nurses, firefighters, and public servants earlier in the day were chanting, 'What do we want, [Prime Minister] Howard's head. How we gonna get it? Tear it off!'

Don't imagine the rioting was just the scuffles shown by Laura Tingle. Weapons used by the rioters included rocks, sticks, cans, paint bombs, a sledge hammer, a wheel brace used to smash glass partitions, a steel shop-trolley, diluted acid, and most fearsome of all, Paul Kelly's 794-page tome *The End of Certainty*, stolen from the gift shop and lobbed at the police lines like a mortar round. One rioter tried to trigger the fire sprinkler system with a lighter. Ninety police and Parliamentary security people were injured — lacerations, sprains, and head and eye injuries. At least a couple were hospitalised. Academic thesis-writer Luke Deer commented, "This was inevitable as two tightly packed groups of several hundred rammed against each other for nearly two hours."

The then-deputy opposition leader Gareth Evans afterwards described the protesters as "crazy, self-indulgent bastards" adding that "what happened yesterday was ugly, un-Australian, stupid and indefensible."

Nurses treated about 40 of the injured, amid blood spatterings on the marble floor and walls, maybe rhyming with the famous first-aid scene in *Gone With the Wind*. The nurses were aided in their ministrations by Trish Worth (Liberal MHR, Adelaide) and a woman, probably with a nursing background, who had been showing off the Great Hall to her doubtless-bemused American guests.

The rioting was to the distant accompaniment of Solidarity Forever and the Internationale, sung by the ACTU choir at the official demo a little down the road.

Constable Rachel Benthein said the protesters she faced had violent motives: "Most of those involved in the assault weren't there to demonstrate against John Howard — they were there to cause destruction and, on the second day, to have a conflict with police." Constable Corey Heldon was part of the police group swept away by the initial charge toward Parliament House: "We ended up against the wrong side of the front doors. The mood was very aggressive, very angry. I've never seen anything like it … They tried to pull me into the crowd but I was pulled back by fellow officers, otherwise I might have been swallowed up by the crowd."

A female officer was allegedly abused and kicked on the ground. Another female officer collapsed as she was crushed between the wall of protesters and police. A security officer also said that at least two female protesters collapsed in the crush. One was passed over the police lines, the other over the protesters.

ACTU Secretary Bill Kelty said the Cavalcade was 'the most successful rally in the history of this country in Canberra'. According to Deer in his thesis, Kelty did not have a detailed knowledge of the events when he made his comments.

The battle was a day before the Howard government brought down its annual budget in a session targeting industrial relations changes. The union armies' transport included a Sydney train re-christened the "Spirit of Protest" — a half-witty play on the venerable Spirit of Progress — and 47 buses just for NSW members of the AMWU.

The rioters, including a high proportion of women, were led by full-time paid union organisers, as named and depicted later in the Sydney Morning Herald's front page. As if that heinous assault on our most sacred democratic institution the Parliament were not enough, Aboriginal activists rioted further the following day at Old Parliament House. If you were an adult in 1996, but can't recall those twin riots, I'm not surprised because bad behaviour by leftists and protected classes goes straight down the media's memory hole. The 7.30 report last night was an exception, driven, I'd say, by the need for some action footage.

On that evening in 1996, ABC TV news held its nose as it pretended to report the vandalism and violence by its political mates. Of that 4.40 minutes coverage, their ABC tribe was more preoccupied with disputing the newly-elected Howard's policies, and petitions against the policies, than describing the trashing of our billion-dollar democratic edifice and injuring of 90 police and guards. As the ABC's then news pundit Jim Middleton put it mildly, "It was the demonstration that got away ... the Opposition's concern is that today's wild scenes have played into the government's hands, diminishing broader public concern about tomorrow's axe-wielding budget." ACTU President Jennie George was quoted, "I regret anything that has occurred but I certainly don't bear the responsibility for it. Thank you." Contrast that with the ABC TV's rabid reporting last week of the Capitol violence, preceded by an ABC placard, "Day of Shame."

After the local riot, Senate President Margaret Reid told the House on August 20 1996 that the "disgraceful and totally unjustifiable" ugly and violent display was "one of the most shameful in this nation's political history."

A peaceful demonstration around Parliament against industrial relations changes had been authorised, with the ACTU taking responsibility for its orderliness. The protest rally remained peaceful until about 12.20 p.m., when a separate group of marchers entered the parliamentary precincts. This group refused to accept police direction, forced a breach in police lines and ran towards the main front entrance of Parliament House. Unfortunately, it was apparent that some of these demonstrators were affected by alcohol. This group was supported by participants from the more general demonstration who were incited to join those involved in riotous conduct by a speaker from the official platform.

Police formed a protective line along the perimeter of the Great Verandah which was subsequently forced back to the main doors. The police line was withdrawn from this area due to the level of violence being experienced by officers, and was redeployed to an area inside the front doors in support of parliamentary security personnel. This deployment stabilised the situation for a short period.

However, demonstrators using increasing force broke through the first line of doors. Once inside this area, demonstrators used weapons, including a large hammer, a wheel brace, a steel trolley and a stanchion torn from the external doors to break open the internal doors. Simultaneously, a second group of demonstrators used other weapons to break into the Parliament House shop, but were held at the internal doors.

The shop was ransacked by demonstrators and major damage was caused by persons who subsequently occupied the area.

PART III

After some two hours, the demonstrators were finally repelled from Parliament House and driven back onto the forecourt area and, shortly afterwards, they dispersed. In addition to the events which took place at the front entrance to the building, incidents also occurred on the Members Terrace, the roof of the Great Verandah and the Queens Terrace.

There were 197 Australian Federal Police on duty at the start of the demonstration, in addition to the Australian Protective Service officers and parliamentary security personnel. A further 60 Australian Federal Police reinforcements were called out under established contingency plans.

The outrageous events which took place yesterday resulted in not only financial but, more importantly and lamentably, human costs. So far about 90 personnel have reported injuries—including lacerations, sprains, and head and eye injuries. I understand one person required hospitalisation.

An initial indicative estimate of the damage to the forecourt and the foyer is up to $75,000. The full extent of looting and criminal damage which resulted from the occupation of the Parliament House shop has yet to be determined.

Finally, I want to apologise most sincerely to the Australian people and those from overseas who were visiting Parliament House and were unfortunately involved, inconvenienced, frightened or shocked in any way by this deplorable incident. To them I say: what you witnessed here yesterday is not typical of Australia or Australians. And I believe I speak for all my colleagues when I say: we hope and pray it never will be.

Local Trots and ferals were unimpressed. One wrote in a feature in *Marxist Left Review*: "As long as capitalism exists, the exploited and the oppressed will fight back in one way or another. Riots will not go away. They are an elemental form of revolt that needs to be supported by all those who hate the current rotten system."

When Jennie George of the ACTU was asked by Nine's Sunday TV show about allegations that union organisers, "paid by the union movement", participated in the riot, she claimed they 'were on their own'. Deer concludes, "The effect of news footage and reports of Jennie George's concerns about the riot reinforced the view that the Government was correct in its condemnation of the ACTU and the labour movement generally." But his own view is, "The ACTU chose to condemn the rioters, rather than the Government for creating the situation." Two years later, Ms George was gonged as one of Australia's "100 living treasures". She was parachuted into a safe seat (Throsby NSW) in 2001 and got her AO in 2013.

Deer in his 1998 Honors thesis called the riots "the most forceful physical attack on the Federal Parliament in Australian history." He was then at the ANU Political Science Department. Despite some of his Marxist-theory pontificating, one can get from him many gems of fact about the affray. Deer makes the fine distinction that the attack was not against the country's key democratic institution, the Parliament; but just against the building which housed the Government (President Trump ought to adopt this line). He relates how the first column on the Commonwealth Avenue ramp was led by a "prominent Aboriginal land campaigner" and his contingent, followed by the CFMEU and students.

Contrary to the authorised plan, they moved in towards the Parliament against riot police opposition.

"At that point ACT CPSU Secretary, Catherine Garvan [Community and Public Sector Union], called out on the public address system on the main stage that the police were trying to block the Aboriginal protesters from reaching the main demonstration and started a chant to 'Let them through'. Protesters from the main rally began to stream towards the point of conflict."

The police had left the Parliament forecourt vulnerable and backed off to protect the entrance. Think Isandlwana and the Zulu hordes, as the police retreated further to the redoubt behind the main doors. Deer writes:

> *Many more demonstrators continued to arrive from the main rally. Protesters forced open the first set of main doors and the police retreated inside the foyer of the building where they attempted to reinforce the second set of doors ... This march of several thousands proceeded to join what seemed to be the main demonstration on the forecourt. One journalist called it 'The unstoppable passing parade'.*

Deer doesn't buy the story that the rioters were just a small minority vis a vis a peaceful 20,000-plus unionists.

> *Indeed several thousand people, if not the majority of the rally, appear to have participated in this activity ... At least 2000 protesters were actively involved in pushing against police lines or directly supporting the act. Thousands of other demonstrators also filled the forecourt and supported the hoisting of banners and*

flags on the building.

He writes that for most of the time demonstrators were separated from police by heavily reinforced steel and glass doors. They tried to force the doors with their bodies. Later they used a trolley from the Parliament House Shop to force open five of the main doors. These gaps were soon filled by police with riot shields. Police attempted to make arrests and protesters tried to break the police line. Punches were exchanged. A number of demonstrators "crowd surfed" over the police line, spurred on by huge cheers from the rioters, but they were quickly arrested by police.

Some demonstrators entered the Parliament House Shop by smashing its glass doors with a wheel brace. They looted teaspoons, tea towels, books and other memorabilia. Some rioters demurred. "It would be wrong to suggest that material gain was the main or even a significant factor explaining the riot," Deer writes.

An empty beer can from the scene allegedly bore a sticker which said "Time to f**k the system that's been f***ing us". The sticker also invited the drinker to throw the can at "anyone who represents the system" and featured a picture of John Howard with an axe buried in his head, "The best cut of all". Deer quotes a facetious Canberra Times journo, Ian Warden, "There were huge cheers as [an effigy of Liberal minister Amanda] Vanstone caught on fire. An angry young man emerged from the cheering crowd to smash in her smoking wire and paper skull again and again with the full force of his skateboard."

Deer says that the rally organisers at the official platform (a big truck) seemed oblivious to the riot just a few hundred metres away. Speakers included the Leader of the ALP Opposition, Kim Beazley, and ACTU President, Jennie George chaired proceedings. Beazley told the baying crowd how the Coalition 'hated' workers, the unemployed, pensioners, students and Aboriginal people. Strangely, the ABC at the time didn't feel that was incitement. Jennie George said that workers were "relying on Labor and the minor parties to defend their rights by defeating the Government's proposals in the Senate". Each time George mentioned 'defeating' she was greeted with huge cheers. Deer wrote, "George's message to the minor party senators was that 'the Australian community will support you in your efforts to defeat this legislation'."

Interrupting the official speeches, Davie Thomason, an Adelaide CFMEU organiser, climbed onto the stage and with bloodied face demanded to speak. Shaking a captured police riot shield, he said: "Brothers and sisters, 100 of us have got into our House. And look what we got from the coppers. And we have to remember it's going to be a long haul but these people up here will never defeat us ... Workers, united, will never be defeated."

Not all ALP federal politicians rushed diplomatically to condemn the onslaught. Deer writes, "Police allege that ALP Senator Rosemary Crowley was in the crowd twenty metres from the doors on the August 19, 'yelling that it was everyone's Parliament House and that everyone should be let in. If people had placards they could just pass them through the security machine and take them inside'. Senator Crowley denied the allegations. The other exception was the Western Australian Greens Senator, Dee Margetts, who suggested that the riot had become a 'law and order' issue "which was being used to mask a more fundamental violence in society."

Deer gives credence to evidence the riot was premeditated by 'hardline Maoists' in the CFMEU.

> *They were joined by 'troublemakers' among the Aboriginal contingent. These were involved in the initial conflict, and in further violence at Old Parliament House the following day. Also jumping on the bandwagon were a range of political extremists – Trotskyite groups and anarchists. These three groups hijacked the event and caused the bulk of the destruction. Through their actions and encouragement these agitators managed to embroil a larger group of unsuspecting protesters in the riot. Combined they formed a violent mob.*

One CFMEU official suggested that 'insurgent student activists' had 'disguised themselves in union shirts and caps'. As mentioned, the Trump camp now is also alleging 'false flag' provocateurs.

A Canberra participant from Mount Bromlow NSW, explained (emphasis added):

> *I am appalled at the white-washing of the event as simple thuggery and the action of a minority of protesters. Everybody seems to be upset that the symbol of democracy, Parliament House, was challenged.* **But it was precisely because it was the seat of government that it was attacked** ... *the busting of the main doors was both a symbolic and*

real challenge to the ivory tower of political power.

I hate to pick at old scabs, but "progressives" were at it again in 2012, this time involving a near assault on the Australian Prime Minister Julia Gillard and Opposition Leader Tony Abbott, who were at an Australia Day celebration at The Lodge restaurant, Canberra. Mainly-Aboriginal rioters besieged The Lodge posing a threat to break down the doors and endanger the politicians. Julia Gillard's bodyguards and federal police had to literally carry her through a howling mob to safety. She lost a shoe on that trip, Evdokia Petrov-fashion, subsequently seized and brandished by rioters. Irony of ironies, the riot was instigated by a staffer in Julia Gillard's own office, who intended only Abbott as the target. The staffer resigned forthwith, departing abruptly overseas for several years of media-free sojourn in UK and Europe before returning to well-paid employment as a Federal Labor apparatchik.

I can hardly wait for Laura Tingle to re-use clips from that episode. Her commentary could go: "Prime Minister Gillard goes high while misogynist Tony Abbott looks at his watch. The Prime Minister's remaining stylish shoe is by Manolo Blahnik."#

Leigh Sales' Most Disgraceful, Biased Interview

16 September 2020

Leigh Sales on the ABC TV's 7.30 last night "interviewed" Donald Trump's former press secretary, Sarah Huckabee Sanders. Sales packed into eight minutes all conceivable ABC bias, venom and hatred of a US President now polling 51 per cent, according to the latest Rassmussen profile of the electorate — a figure reflecting support before the signing of the twin Israeli peace deals with UAE and Bahrain. No wonder the ABC experts all got the 2016 Trump election wrong. That's what happens when Sales and her ilk isolate in their Trump-derangement cocoon.

In 100 per cent "gotcha" questioning, Sales called Sanders every kind of liar, sleaze and religious hypocrite. Sanders should have walked off but instead took on the ABC compere. She blasted back at the mainstream media and its pro-Democrat lies, epitomised by the media's two years of phony Russia-collusion scoops. Sales' ABC pal, Sarah Ferguson is infamous for her three-part bombshell-that-wasn't "story of the century" in 2018 endorsing the fake "collusion" narrative.

Sales had no answer to Sanders' ripostes and continued to read from her vituperative question-list. After suggesting Sanders was a ratbag for about the fourth time in under eight minutes, Sales had the gall to demand that Sanders in reply stick to her questions-cum-accusations.

Sales, the ABC's $400,000-or-so princess, has previously

spent interview-time licking the toes of now-disgraced anti-Trumpers James Comey the FBI chief (19/4/18), Hillary Clinton (May 14, 2018), and only last week, octogenarian actress Jane Fonda, who began bawling on camera while contemplating the death of this heat-ravaged planet as global warming does its worst. Fonda the one-time exercise queen would have been better off chatting to a qualified medical professional.

But back to Sanders, whom Sales quizzed about Trump's notorious 'pussy-grabbing' comment of 2005, but she didn't put questions to Hillary along similar lines. Had she done so, the exchange would have gone like this:

> *"Why did you organise a defence of your husband Bill based on calling his rape-accusers 'nuts and sluts', and how did you feel when you learnt your Presidential husband had inserted a cigar into a young intern's vagina in the Oval Office?"*

Those questions would have been followed up with the reprimand barked at Sanders, *"Mrs Clinton, you are not addressing my questions."*

Here's a sample of the actual interview:

> LEIGH SALES: *Somebody who has watched 30-plus years of your career would see extreme hours, high pressure, sexism, relentless public attacks, loss of privacy…*
>
> HILLARY CLINTON *(laughs)*: *Ooh, sounds pretty horrible, doesn't it? (Laughs)*
>
> SALES (laughs): *Well, and then, you know: also at the end a brutal exit.*

CLINTON: *Yes.*

SALES: *What would you say to people who look at your experience and go: "Well, there's just ... it's not worth it: going into public life."*

Similarly, Sales has launched no follow-up of her political infatuation with James Comey to disclose his mis-use and lying about the fake "Steele [Russian pee] dossier". Comey used the dossier to enable FBI spying on the Trump 2015 election campaign, and also authorised the entrapment of now-vindicated Trump executive Lt Gen Michael Flynn. That was the Deep State in action.

Sales' interview of climate hysteric Jane Fonda was also deeply respectful, even when her guest lamented that she had only one servant in her $US5.4m Los Angeles mansion.

SALES: *Because of your activism, you've attracted plenty of controversy. A lot of people dislike you; they have strong opinions about you. Has that been hard to take?*

Now let's get specific. Sales' first question to Sanders was: "Can Donald Trump tell the difference the truth and a lie?" The basis for Sales' insult was that the *Washington Post* claims to have fact-checked presidential statements and found some 20,000 alleged lies by the President. It didn't occur to Sales that WaPo, with *The New York Times*, has proudly thrown objectivity overboard to help Biden oust Trump.

Sales next question was another beaut:

PART III

> *This isn't from the media, this is from General Colin Powell, the US Secretary of State during the last Republican administration; 'He has not been an effective President. He lies all the time. He began lying the day of the Inauguration, and I don't think that's in our interest. The situation in 2020 has gotten worse.'*

Fact Check on Sales: Republican Powell? Come off it, lady. Powell is the John Hewson of American politics, the liberal touted by progressives as a conservative. Powell endorsed Barack Obama's presidential bids in 2008 and 2012 and boasted of voting for Hillary Clinton in 2016. He has pledged to vote for Biden in November and is campaigning hard against Trump. Please mention all this next time you trot out Powell as your Republican source.

Third question from Sales:

> *Let me give you an example from yesterday in a discussion about the California wildfires. The State Secretary for Natural Resources pointed out America has recently recorded some of its hottest temperatures on record and that is a factor in the severity of the fires, along with land management. The President replied, 'It will start getting cooler.' The Secretary replied, 'I wish science agreed with you.' The President then replied, 'I don't think science knows actually.'*
>
> *Was that a display of lying, ignorance or insanity?*

While Sales is a lioness tackling an ex-press secretary across the seas, I can't imagine her similarly clawing Premier Dan Andrews, for example, about his lie — one of so very, very many — that curfews were medically recommended: 'Mr Andrews, was that a display of lying, ignorance or insanity?' In any event, Sales' question to Sanders was not genuinely seeking an answer. It merely involved an ABC tax-paid reporter getting up on her soapbox, to the applause of her in-house coterie.

Second of all, as the Americans say, Sales makes a fool of herself with her climate assumptions. California, like the rest of the planet, has warmed 1degC or a bit more in the past 100 years. Of that, only some fraction is anthropogenic warming. In California especially, the "heat island effect" has grown with the state's development. Where sites have stayed obstinately rural, temperatures have shown much less rise than 1degC. It is ridiculous to cite a puny, human-caused heating of under 1degC in a century as the cause of the wildfires when lax forest management was admitted this week by California's Governor himself.

Third, no-one knows the future and if Trump says we'll get cooling, there's ample scientific justification, including the sunspot impact on climate being now the weakest since the Dalton Minimum in the Little Ice Age in late 18th century. The warmist scientists never predicted the warming hiatus after 2000, and they might (or might not) be wrong again. Warming predictions are based on models prone to the garbage-in/garbage-out syndrome, as with COVID-19 models. Sales might be astounded by Trump's statement, "I don't think the science knows, actually" but any honest scientist would give Trump five stars.

Sales next question or speech ran like this:

PART III

So to believe you, somebody watching this interview has to believe that every former senior member of the Trump administration who has left and spoken of his unfitness to lead has an axe to grind, that every former senior Republican who has spoken out, from Colin Powell to the late John McCain, has an axe to grind, and then all of these life-long Republicans are in cahoots with the Democrats and they're all also tied up in a conspiracy with the mainstream media and it's the mainstream media that's peddling lie after lie, not Donald Trump? That's what you're asking people to believe?

Powell, as I showed above, is very definitely "in cahoots with the Democrats". As for McCain, Sales again fails to do her homework: Senator McCain was also "in cahoots" with the Democrats. In 2013 he was part of a "gang of eight" including Democrat senators who pursued soft policies on illegal immigrants, and in 2016 he joined Democrats in calling for the Russia-collusion inquiry into Trump. To cap it off, in 2017 he cast the pivotal vote with Democrats to block Trump's repeal of Obamacare.

Next unpack: Sales can't believe that Trump ex-executives would tittle-tattle to the media (she needs to get out more) and yes, the media (especially her ABC) does lie to defame Trump. Close to home, I caught out an ABC reporter lying that Trump had called COVID-19 a hoax, and the ABC corrections team had to agree and post a correction.

Is she not even aware that an NYT staffer taped executive editor Dean Baquet lecturing staff a year ago, after an uproar because a sub-editor had used a neutral rather than an anti-Trump headline after a mass shooting:

> It got trickier after [inaudible] ... went from being a story about whether the Trump campaign had colluded with Russia and obstruction of justice to being a more head-on story about the president's character. We built our newsroom to cover one [fake] story, and we did it truly well. Now we have to regroup, and shift resources and emphasis to take on a different story. I'd love your help with that.

Baquet also remarked, "What I'm saying is that our readers and some of our staff cheer us when we take on Donald Trump, but they jeer at us when we take on Joe Biden."

In other words, the Trump collusion beat-up flopped, so the NYT shifted to smearing Trump on other fronts, with the editor needing from reporters a further line of attack.

Next Sales question:

> Your book makes it clear that you're heavily guided by your Christian faith and family values. How do you reconcile that with having been the spokesperson for a President who has misled the American people on everything from coronavirus to climate change, who boasts about grabbing women on the pussy, who paid hush money to a porn star to keep her quiet about their alleged relationship and who has maligned the men and women of America's armed forces?

SANDERS: *Well, some of those things are just patently false.*

SALES: *They're not actually.*

[TONY THOMAS: *They are false, actually*].

Sales appears to refer to the Bob Woodward book allegations that Trump deliberately played down COVID-19. The top medico Dr Fauci denies that Trump misled the public. Trump also made numerous statements emphasising the virulency of the virus. Woodward's claims are not only many months' stale, but themselves misleading.

Pussy-grabbing talk? True. Hush money, true. Maligning the armed forces? The "suckers and losers" alleged quotes were nothing but a Democrat/media hit job based on anonymous smears in the face of attributed denials by several/many senior people present at the time. Sales' ABC pal David Lipson endorsed the anonymous smears on 7pm news and I've complained to the ABC about this bias (no response yet).

> SALES TO SANDERS: *I notice you're not addressing the central premise of my question which is how somebody like Donald Trump squares with the values you espouse?*

Sales using Sanders' Christian faith as a stick to beat her with is disgusting. Her question, again, is not a question but a stump speech. As a thought-experiment, imagine Sales interviewing Joe Biden as follows: *'Mr Biden, last March your staffer Tara Reade alleged you sexually assaulted her. We in the mainstream media have for years run cover for you over Reade's claims but here's what Wikipedia reports:*

> In a March 25, 2020, interview with Katie Halper, Reade alleged that Biden had pushed her against a wall, kissed her, put his hand under her skirt, penetrated her with

his fingers, and asked, "Do you want to go somewhere else?" Reade told National Public Radio(NPR) for an April 19 article, "His hands went underneath my clothing and he was touching me in my private areas and without my consent." Reade told The Intercept her impression was that Biden believed he had consent and was surprised when she rejected him. Reade told The New York Times for an April 12 article that when she pulled away from Biden, he looked puzzled and said, "Come on, man, I heard you liked me." She then said he told her "You're nothing to me, nothing," followed by "You're OK, you're fine."

Mr Biden, how do you reconcile such alleged behaviour, which has multiple corroborations, with your Catholic faith, and by the way, aren't you in favor of abortion?

Here is Sales' next question to Sanders (real):

After the FBI director, James Comey, was fired, as White House spokesperson you said that countless members of the FBI had told the Trump administration, they had no confidence in him.

Under oath to the Mueller investigation, you admitted that was not founded on anything, a slip of the tongue, and said, "In the heat of the moment."

How often did you have those kinds of slips of the tongue, in the heat of the moment as White House spokesperson?

Sanders replied, acknowledging her mistake and apologising. "I had heard from a number of members of the FBI, both current and former, but I said I shouldn't have used that particular word [countless]."

Sales in mid-sentence did her own "slip of the tongue" in the "heat of the moment". Sanders corrected Sales that she was not "under oath" to the investigation, but giving a "voluntary interview". She has consistently clarified that she should have referred to "some" rather than "countless" FBI officials.

The interview reminded me of that movie, "The Lady and the Tramp". Which of the two women cited here was which? #

PART IV: HISTORY BITS AND PIECES

Freeman Dyson's War by Numbers

9 March, 2020

My science hero is Richard Feynman, but his understudy, Freeman Dyson, who died on 28 February 2020, runs a close second. To him maths came as naturally as breathing. At the age of four he was trying to calculate the number of atoms in the sun. By 15 at Winchester College he was teaching himself Russian to read the best book on number theory, by Ivan Vinogradov.

At about 24, he obtained two letters supporting his switch from Cambridge to join nuclear physicist Hans Bethe's group at Cornell University. One letter said he was "not completely stupid" and the other more generously called him "the best mathematician in Britain."

His climate scepticism was a thorn in the side of orthodox climate scientists. As Arnis Rītups put it in a long piece in a Latvian journal four years ago,

> In the last decade Dyson has become one of the most authoritative voices to assert that 'global warming' is first of all not global (it is limited to the cold regions, winter and night time) and second,

> *there is no scientific evidence that it is dangerous, and third, that the related ideology and propaganda turns people's attention away from much more pressing problems.*

Presciently, Ritups asked him

> *It's a strange fact of human life that thinking about one's death somehow intensifies one's life. Do you have an explanation for this close relationship between consciousness and death?*

To which Dyson replied:

> *No, I don't think I would say I have an explanation. It's certainly common sense that if life went on forever it would be very boring. (Laughs.) It would be very boring to have to go through the same routines over and over forever. I think it's a practical matter. Certainly, human society absolutely depends on people dying. If everybody were still around, there would be nothing much for the young people to do. (Laughs.)*

I was cheered by this excellent interview, especially Dyson's view that even nuclear war wouldn't destroy humanity and civilisation. Incidentally, as well as winning top science prizes, Freeman also won the Templeton Prize in 2000 for progress in religion.

> *Dyson: "I think it's very hard for us humans to destroy ourselves. It's not as easy as people imagine."*

> *Ritups: How come?*

> *Dyson: Well, because we are extraordinarily resilient.*

PART IV

Ritups: Like rats, you mean?

Dyson: Yes. Probably rats and humans are about equally good. (Laughs.)

Ritups: Well, that gives us some basis for optimism about the future.

Dyson: Yes! When you look at the possible ways we can destroy ourselves you'd think nuclear war would be the most likely to wipe us out. But if you look at a real nuclear war ... Of course, it would destroy all the cities, which would be sad for all sorts of people—there's no doubt it would be a huge disaster—but there would still be a lot of villages left where people would hardly notice. There would be places that happened to not get radiated. When you have a lot of radiation in the air it mostly comes to the ground via rains. So if you happen to be in a place where it's not raining, you're lucky. Also if you happen to live in a cave, even a few feet underground, it reduces the radiation very strongly. So it's very hard to imagine there wouldn't be lots of humans surviving. And, of course, it takes only a few to start the species all over again.

Freeman, a most kind and upright man, spent the war years from 1943 in Operational Research calculating how to make Bomber Command more efficient at obliterating German cities, preferably by firestorms. He was only 19-20. To take his mind off his job, he created proofs in pure mathematics which later earned him a berth at Trinity College. He switched to particle physics because it offered harder problems.

I'm a World War Two buff and particularly interested in his work for Bomber Command. I've drawn heavily on his 6000-word essay *A Failure of Intelligence*. By statistical reasoning Dyson found that to minimise air casualties the Lancasters should be stripped of gun turrets and fly packed densely together, despite the risk of collisions. Such a policy would enable the planes to fly higher and 50mph faster to evade night fighters, and spend less time over Germany's flak belts. The turrets did not save bombers, because the gunners rarely saw the fighters that killed them. He found an ally in Air Vice-Marshal Sir Ralph Cochrane, commander of 5 Group. Freeman writes in his book, *Dreams of Earth and Sky*, "Being a flamboyant character, he planned to rip out the Lancaster's gun turrets and all the associated dead weight, ground the two gunners, and paint the whole thing white. Then he would fly it over Germany, so high and so fast that nobody could shoot him down." He was overruled and the white Lancaster never flew.

Dyson also verified statistically that crews' chance of survival on missions did not increase with experience. About 75 per cent of crew never completed their 30-ops tours, but which of the planes were shot down turned out to be entirely random. The RAF was having none of it. First, crew morale would suffer if there were no gunners to provide at least the illusion of hitting back at night fighters. Second, crews on just about every trip saw, or thought they saw, collisions. And third, crews needed to believe that more experience made them safer after each trip.

Freeman was in a team based in trailers behind Bomber Command's main headquarters building in Buckinghamshire. He says the Germans must have known about the buildings but never tried to bomb them. Billeted in a nearby village and provided with the classic English weekly bath, he biked uphill five miles to work and coasted home after knock-off.

Bomber command was absorbing a quarter of the entire British war effort. "Sometimes, as I was struggling up the hill, an Air Force limousine would zoom by, and I would have a quick glimpse of our commander in chief, Sir Arthur Harris sitting in the back, on his way to give the orders that sent thousands of boys my age to their deaths."

Dyson and the 30 other Operations Research people remained civilians, giving independent scientific/technical advice to top commanders. The system had spun off from a Royal Navy model, testing whether claimed U-Boat sinkings were valid. "Every ship or airplane that dropped a depth charge somewhere near a U-boat was apt to claim a kill," Dyson says. His statistics involved assessing bomber damage and losses, with peripheral work on electronic counter-measures. The uniformed women auxiliaries did most of the real work and made a depressing situation bearable. "Their leader was Sergeant Asplen, a tall and strikingly beautiful girl whose authority was never questioned. The sergeant kept herself free of romantic entanglements."

His first day at work followed the initial use of the Window device on a Hamburg raid. This involved crew throwing out strips of paper coated with aluminium paint to confuse German radar's ability to guide night fighters to individual bombers. The team was joyful: losses were only 12 out of 791 bombers, or 1.5 per cent rather than the regular 5 per cent. Window had saved about 180 of our boys that night, he noted.

The attacks on Hamburg continued for his first week, with the second raid generating a firestorm that killed 40,000. Normally civilians bivouacked underground and even a big raid was likely to kill "only" a few thousand. But a firestorm suffocated or roasted everyone underground as well. The RAF succeeded in creating only one other firestorm, in Dresden in 1945, which killed 25,000-60,000.

Freeman eventually decided that firestorms only occurred where buildings were dense, incendiaries fell in concentrated areas, and atmospheric conditions were right. The Americans managed one in Tokyo –100,000 killed.

The Germans quickly countered Window by ignoring individual bombers and guiding their night fighters into the stream itself. Loss rates within a month hit 5 per cent again. Meanwhile, Freeman continued to verify statistically the collision rate – not easy when two out of three collisions over Germany left no survivors. Not surprisingly, aircrews liked to quit the tight formations for fear of collisions. They would see in the distance broken bombers tumbling to earth, even when night fighters were absent. Moreover, the crews were constantly having what they saw as near-misses.

PART IV

The bombers corkscrewed to throw off anti-aircraft guns, weaving up and down and side-to-side. The parameters of Freeman's collision formulae were wildly variable but he was at least able to say the maximum collision rate would be about 1 per cent, well below the total loss per operation of 5 per cent. "Even if we squeezed the bomber stream to the highest possible density, collisions would not be the main cause of losses," he observed.

Freeman enjoyed interviewing crew who survived collisions and returned. One odd case was a pair of those fast wooden Mosquitos whose pilots were so confident they collided while staging a mock dogfight over Munich.

The real culprit in losses was the German system coded *Shraege Musik*, translated as 'crooked music' or sometimes Jazz. This involved night fighters creeping below a bomber's blind spot and dousing the plane with cannon installed to fire 60deg upwards. Freeman: "This system efficiently destroyed thousands of bombers, and we did not even know that it existed. This was the greatest failure of the Operations Research. We learned about it too late to do anything to counter it."

The German system also accounted for much of the finding that crews were shot down regardless of their experience. "I blame [his team], and I blame myself in particular, for not taking this result seriously enough," Freeman wrote. "The evidence showed that the main cause of losses was an attack that gave experienced crews no chance either to escape or to defend themselves. If we had taken the evidence more seriously, we might have discovered

Schräge Musik in time to respond with effective countermeasures."

Freeman interviewed survivors whose planes had been shot up. Most had never seen the fighter and had no warning of an attack. There was just a sudden burst of cannon fire, and the aircraft fell apart around them. "Again, we missed an essential clue that might have led us to *Schräge Musik*."

Some of his work had a null result. The RAF had installed a tail-mounted device called Monica. When Monica picked up an object behind, it squealed over the intercom. Crews disliked all the false alarms and turned it off so they could use the intercom. Freeman had to answer whether Monica was useful. For this he invented a form of 'meta-analysis', later a standard technique in epidemiology and drug trials. The crews were right – Monica was useless.

Everyone knows that the RAF won the Battle of Britain but Freeman describes how the RAF lost the aerial Battle of Berlin.

'Bomber' Harris started the Battle of Berlin in 1943 to prove that he could bomb Germany out of the war. The first 444-bomber raid in November was a success with only nine planes lost. This was not because of Window but from misleading the German controllers to mis-route their fighters to Mannheim. Fifteen big attacks followed in 1943 and 1944, none very successful. The reasons included cloudy weather and strengthened defences. In the final attack the RAF lost a horrific 72 bombers out of 791, or 9 per cent. The Germans knew well the routes of the bomber streams and the fighters were knocking down bombers all the way.

PART IV

In total, the Berlin campaign cost 492 bombers and 3,000 aircrew, with no serious disruption to Berlin's industry.

One of Freeman's colleagues, Sebastian Pease, escaped from the headquarters trailers and spent his time with 218 Stirling Squadron in the field. Freeman only found out what Pease was doing 50 years later. He was coaching aircrews in a precise navigation system called G-H, requiring two-way communication with ground stations. It was fitted to slow and obsolete Stirling bombers which could then do small precision raids. "The rest of us were sitting at Command Headquarters, depressed and miserable because our losses of aircraft and aircrew were tremendous and we were unable to do much to help."

In early 1944, 218 Squadron stopped bombing and began training for a super-secret D-Day component called GLIMMER. This involved Stirlings flying low, tight circles over the channel and dropping Window, in conjunction with special shipping. The scheme tricked the German radar into "seeing" a phantom invasion fleet heading for Pas de Calais while the real fleet was bound for Normandy, 200 miles west. Apropos of Pease's 50-year silence, Freeman's boss, Reuben Smeed, once said, "In this business, you have a choice. Either you get something done or you get the credit for it, but not both." Smeed went on to civilian work globally on intelligent traffic-light systems.

Freeman's group was sickened by the Dresden raids but the British public was all for bringing the war home to German civilians.

Dyson: "I remember arguing about the morality of city bombing with the wife of a senior air force officer, after the Dresden attack. She was a well-educated and intelligent woman who worked part-time for Operational Research. I asked her whether she really believed that it was right to kill German women and babies in large numbers at that late stage of the war. She answered, 'Oh yes. It is good to kill the babies especially. I am not thinking of this war but of the next one, 20 years from now. The next time those babies will be the soldiers.'"

After fighting Germans for ten years, four in the first war and six in the second, we had become almost as bloody-minded as Sir Arthur [Harris], wrote Freeman, who speculated that if Britain in 1936 had focused on building ships rather than bombers, it might have invaded France and ended the war a year earlier. "But in 1943, we had the bombers, and we did not have the ships, and the problem was to do the best we could with what we had." #

Battling the Reds in Adelaide

20 December 2019

How many of us were in my Willagee branch of the Communist Party in Perth around 1960? Maybe six or eight. We bonded well but we weren't powerhouses of the intellect. We'd gloat about the impending world revolution, nut out ways to get it started, and then pivot to the contentious stuff – whose turn was it to letterbox Garling Street?

I can now assume one of our tight-knit band was an ASIO informer. From 1956 ASIO's Operation Sparrow aimed to put an agent into every Communist Party branch. The best-known informer is Phil Geri, who kept reporting on the Ballarat branch while its membership declined to four (or maybe five, Geri included).

My mother and stepfather, who did high-level CPA work, were confident that Party vigilance screened out would-be informers. "I can spot one a mile off," my stepfather would say, with a sardonic grin. In reality ASIO riddled the Party with spies, probably to Central Committee level. Once in, they were seldom outed because the Party never thought to check: Who volunteers for dreary tasks? And who pays their Party dues on time? Tick the two boxes and there's your ASIO agent.

My favourite historian is Professor Phil Deery of Victoria University. He specialises in ASIO-CPA relations and refreshes my memories of a politically mis-spent youth. I stumbled across his latest revelations about ASIO's Adelaide spy, Anne Neill, in Labor

History (11/2018), *"A Most Important Cadre": The Infiltration of the Communist Party of Australia during the Early Cold War*. Deery's stuff is too good to lie unread in Labor History, hence I'm giving it an audience here. Thank Deery, not me.

For reasons unexplained, ASIO released 13 files on Anne Neill totalling 2,664 pages, with various redactions. Deery could hardly believe his luck: "On no other agent has anything like this occurred," he writes. (There's several pages about Neill in David Horner's official ASIO history, published in 2014, but it's rather mundane).

Deery's tale is about middle-class, religious and patriotic Adelaide widow Anne Neill. From 1950-58 she was a trusted and hard-working secretary and aide to the Party leaders, slipping an extra carbon sheet into her typewriter roller and embracing what her sister disparaged as "a life of deceit".

She almost wore out Rod Allanson, the agent-runner in ASIO's Adelaide office, a tough character who had survived the Thai-Burma railroad. In 1950 he had slotted her into an unpaid typist job for Elliott Johnston, a top SA and federal Communist who also ran the SA Peace Council front.

Johnston eventually gained some respectability as a Supreme Court Judge and a Royal Commissioner into Aboriginal Deaths in Custody (1987). It is normal for Communists to become judges, although I was somehow overlooked. War-time waterfront slacker and Trotskyite Ken Gee (aka "Comrade Roberts") later graced the bench of the NSW District Court for a decade.

Anne Neill's career and my own do have some eerie parallels. Her first undercover job was to help run the Stockholm Peace Appeal of 1950 to ban atom bombs. Like Neill I gathered signatures, corrupting ten-year-old playmates at Nedlands Primary School. Neill and I helped generate the purported Australian tally of 200,000 signatures, which in turn helped generate the purported 475m signatures worldwide. That was one in every 40 Australians and one in every five humans in the world. Stalin knew how to get things done.

Two years later, Neill caught the train from Adelaide to represent South Australia at Sydney's Youth Carnival for Peace & Friendship. I did the same from Perth at 12, as WA's youngest delegate, raising high the banner of the Junior Eureka Youth League.

Neill slaved over costumes for the Communists' New Theatre production of the Reedy River musical – it must have toured to Perth, as I can still hum, "Ten miles down Reedy River one Sunday afternoon/I rode with Mary Campbell to that broad, bright lagoon."

That's enough about me. A surveillance photo of Neill in the doorway of Adelaide's "People's Book Shop" shows a dumpy woman about 50 with flimsy white hair, thin lips, a strong jaw and a determined expression. Her main concession to femininity is a whitish necklace topping her baggy cotton dress.

As one Party person put it, "Comrade Anne – it beats me how she gets through all the work she does. She makes costumes for the opera, is in charge of costumes for the New Theatre, makes jars of pickles and marmalades for Party fairs, as well as writes letters and is Secretary of other organisations."

By late 1952 ASIO was calling her its "most prolific source", as she supplied a succession of three agent-runners with hundreds of reports rated highest-grade. One case officer noted that her morale was "surprisingly high" and that she was an "absolute inspiration".

ASIO's Allanson recalled, "Anne Neill was so active that she demanded much of my time and attention. And when I had finished my normal day's work, I found it necessary to have clandestine meetings with her, night after night, so that I could record all the detail she provided and also brief her on further action required."

She was raised a devout Christian by conservative and imperial-minded parents and took on her spy role as a responsible citizen keeping track of subversives as a duty to her country and the Crown. She tracked not only the Party and the Peace Council, but at least seven other Communist fronts such as the Union of Australian Women and Realist Writers' Group. At times she would be at their meetings seven nights a week.

She fooled the Party largely because she looked so guileless – "the middle-aged lady with the beautiful, innocent blue eyes", as one Party wife recollected. SA Party boss John Sendy found her "well-mannered, unassuming and quite charming" but after she was outed, he modified his assessment: "a b…. [sic] old bitch – she was so nice all the time."

So nice she didn't have to worm her way into the Party, having been told the Party "would be pleased to welcome you". This slack security was when the Party was under siege by Menzies and notwithstanding Neill's previous overt membership of the Liberal & Country League! The Melbourne Herald later called her "a white-haired widow with a kind face. She could be the woman from the house across the corner."

After the Sydney Peace Carnival, she wangled her way onto a deputation to another "Peace Conference" in Peking. She loaded the dice by saying she could pay her own fares, thanks to a £400 insurance payout which in fact was ASIO money. En route she wrote letters to her family disclosing ASIO secrets, which alarmed ASIO when it opened them. The Catholic News-Weekly even quoted one of her travelling companions saying Neill was unsympathetic to Communism – luckily for ASIO, Party leaders didn't read News-Weekly.

When she blabbed to the Australian Trade Commissioner in Hong Kong that she was a secret agent, he thought her claim "outrageous". But she came home with a swag of materials for ASIO on Communist policies, issues and personalities. The Party was just as delighted with their delegate and she was lionised on lecture tours, enthralling the faithful with 90-minute orations. Indeed, her status was so high that the Soviet Embassy in November 1953 gave her a half-hour private audience with Vladimir Petrov. He and wife,

Evdokia, deferred on her invitation to stay with her in Adelaide. Her hob-nobbing backfired when the Petrovs defected in April 1954: Party bigwigs wrongly suspected she had a hand in it.

Without warning they interrogated her twice within two days, probing for holes in her ASIO-provided cover stories. They particularly demanded documents to authenticate her (ASIO-sourced) £400 windfall. While she stalled for time, ASIO alerted her solicitor and another friend to lie about this money if required. Ever scrupulous, ASIO added a marginal note to "make sure this matter is fully insulated so that there is no possible chance of perjury."

Using considerable psychological skills, ASIO briefed her to "Threaten to resign from the CP of A and frontal organisations, and indicate indignation at the continual questioning." Her inquisitor, Elliott Johnston, fell for this ruse, soothing her, "Now, don't be upset, don't get angry, all I want is that written paper to prove where you got that money". The CPA State Secretary, Eddie Robertson, feared she might tell the Party to "get f—" if they pushed her too hard.

Deery writes that Neill's health deteriorated. "Within two days, she had undergone a two-hour grilling, a three-hour briefing with ASIO officers, a long meeting/dinner with Marjorie Johnston (Elliott's wife) that Neill apparently recorded, and the interrogation by the CPA Control Commission." The historian attributes her success to "calm steadfastness in the face of interrogation, the careful handling and shrewd advice by her case officer, and the stonewalling of repeated requests to supply documentary proof."

After a considerable sick spell, she returned to the Party fold and resumed her mind-boggling industriousness, working long hours on costume-making for June's production of Reedy River. Party leaders promoted her to delegate to the State Conference and she spoofed them for a further four years. By mid-1958, however, eight years late, suspicions arose. It was likely through Party women's intuition rather than male Party intellect. A female ASIO agent discovered from the mother of CPA boss John Sendy that Neill had been too darn curious about too many Party issues, and the documents about the £400 had, after all, never been produced. Mrs Sendy said Neill was

> *In everything ... [She] goes about getting information from people and she is so charming and so nice about it ... She gets paid to do it. Actually, I hate mentioning the word, but it is Security ... She was put on to me by Security. She must know that I spoke to John about it ... I did have my suspicions when she came here to pump me [about John Sendy, when he attended a training school in China] ... John said, "Look, Mum, there is nothing we can do at present ... [but] we will hold her back from getting in too far." We know she only gets a widow's pension, yet she can have a trip abroad ... I couldn't do it. How does she do it? She is always ready to pay her payments to the Party. She will give anything to the Party. You or I couldn't do it ... We are watching her closely now. John has suspected her for some time, but it is only recently that he told me that he was now fairly certain about it. The Party*

> had "tried all ways to trap her but we couldn't" and her house was watched for 14 days and nights, "but she wasn't seen."

By this time Neill was religiously involved in the Commonwealth Revival Crusade and boring her case officer with tales about godly revenge on Russia and faith-healing miracles by American evangelist Billy Adams.

Both the CPA and ASIO were happy to see her eased quietly out of Party work. It left quite a gap, as Adelaide by then had fewer than 20 members. ASIO presented her with a pricey cutlery set as a memento. But with her visceral hatred of Communists she spent another three years writing for ASIO scores of highly personal "character studies" of Party figures, up to eight typed pages long. She also rejoined the Liberal & Country League.

In December 1961, in a bizarre denouement, she went public in Adelaide's Daily Mail with tell-all features about her ASIO career, under headings like "Secret Service Housewife", "I Spied for Security", "I Join the Party", "I Go Behind the Iron Curtain"; and "I Talked Alone to Petrov". Sub-headings included "How she tricked the Reds" and "Mixed with top men in Kremlin." The pieces were to be syndicated before the December 1961 election but Sunday Mail editor K.V. Parish held them over until after the election. Menzies scraped home with a one-seat majority. Deery doesn't comment on whether Parish's decision was good or bad form.

Neill's revelations left the Party with an emu egg omelette on its face. ASIO taps recorded bigwigs now calling their Stakhanovite ex-worker a police pimp, traitor, provocateur and shameless stool pigeon. "Personally," stated one Party leader Alan Miller, "I would rather hang myself than do what she has done." Another, Graham Beinke, thought, "It is a pity she is old because by the time Communism comes to Australia she will be dead and we won't be able to do anything to her." There were suggestions of retaliation ranging from psychological pressure to physical violence. These were quickly suppressed by Party leaders, who adopted a wait-and-see policy, Deery writes.

She went on a TV panel but gave rambling answers and factual slips. ASIO was discomfited and for next time, considered that "a prior approach should be made to a trusted, loyal and discreet member of the interviewing panel."

Menzies praised her work and her decision to publish the articles, saying that she'd done a "good service" to Australia because she awakened people to the role of "innocent-looking communist 'front' organisations".

Neill next became a celebrity of the far-right fringe, such as Eric Butler's luridly anti-Semitic League of Rights. She became a Holocaust denier ("Only propaganda – Jewish lies") and Protocols of the Elders of Zion truther. She even alleged that a Zionist was calling the shots top-level within ASIO. Her late years devolved into fantasies about Russian spies and retributions and she went into care in 1980 at age 81.

Deery hedges his bets on whether Neill's unmasking of CPA plots had any point. It depends on whether the "peace movement" was genuinely subversive or merely political, he says. In 1977, Royal Commissioner Robert Hope defined "subversion" to include criminality, severely cramping ASIO's style.

Retrofitting the "criminality" definition, Deery says that little in those many hundreds of Neill's assiduous reports could be regarded as "subversive." With CPA membership in SA totalling only 220 in 1953, Neill and ASIO were tilting at windmills. "Threats to national security from Communist subversion may have existed elsewhere, but not from South Australia in the 1950s," he concludes.

One day ASIO's cutlery gift to Anne will turn up on Antique Roadshow. I'm putting in a bid. #

PART IV

Abe Saffron and the Man From ASIO

10 April 2021

The ABC series on the Ghost Train fire in Sydney's Luna Park was great TV. Congrats to Caro Meldrum-Hanna and her ABC team's 18 months of investigation of the fire. Praise where praise is due.

What a parade of crooks helped in the sleazy cover-up of undoubted arson on June 9, 1979: Inspector Doug Knight, who bulldozed the burnt site within half a day and stymied any forensic work, and his mafia-linked Deputy Police Commissioner Bill Allen who resigned in disgrace three years later. Then we go one step up to the premier who appointed Allen, Neville Wran, and then even higher to Mr Justice Murphy on the High Court. They were all in thrall to NSW's crime czar and mobster Abe 'Boss of the Cross' Saffron.

The ABC program provides evidence that Saffron organised bikies to light the ghost train fire that incinerated one father and six schoolboys. Saffron then secretly acquired the Luna Park real estate, with help from Wran and Lionel Murphy.

One player in the tawdry NSW scene wasn't mentioned in the series: the Australian Security Intelligence Organisation. Through much of Saffron's career, a top ASIO operative, Dudley Doherty, was Saffron's best mate and actually did the mobster's secret accurate accounts, as distinct from the tax accounts. Doherty, when not mole-hunting or spying on communists and their associates, was enjoying Abe's prostitutes in Abe's brothels. As foreplay, he fed the ladies plates of oysters. Doherty died in office in 1970, long before the Ghost Train fire, while Saffron died at 87 in 2006.

Doherty's long-time boss was ASIO chief Sir Charles Spry, who left office the same year Dudley died. His successor was the randy and hopeless Peter Barbour (1970-75) followed by Frank Mahony and Justice Sir Edward Woodward. Did ASIO post-Doherty continue its intimacies with Saffron? Who knows?

Was Doherty a rogue ASIO operative moonlighting for a mobster? Or was his decades-long intimacy with Saffron in the line of ASIO duty? We all know how J. Edgar Hoover controlled US presidents Truman, Nixon and Kennedy through his blackmail-worthy files on their peccadilloes. ASIO's Doherty must have collected for Spry a heap of dirt on top NSW and federal figures, including long-serving and corrupt NSW Premier Robert Askin. (Saffron had been paying Askin and his equally corrupt police commissioner Norm Allen $5000-10,000 a week, in return for protecting his illegal liquor, brothel, loan sharking and gambling activities across mainland Australia. That's as much as $70,000 a week in today's money in Askin's last year – 1975 - in office). Doherty also winked at Saffron's thuggery, crimes, and tax evasion.

You can read the sanitised account of Dudley Doherty and his wife Joan (also an ASIO agent) scattered through the pages of David Horner's 2014 official history of ASIO — Volume 1, The Spy Catchers. Horner celebrated the Dohertys chiefly for the family's role in harbouring the Vladimir and Evdokia Petrov defectors when they were at maximum risk from Soviet assassins during the 1956 Olympics. Joan had also toiled at early and primitive intercepts of Soviet spies' conversations.

Dudley Doherty was also ASIO's lock-picker extraordinaire. Horner relates that Doherty, to pass a special lock-picking course, had to choose an apparently un-pickable lock. He picked the personal safe of ASIO boss Spry and left a note in it, "which did not go down well with Spry". However author Sandra Hogan, quoting the family, says the safe belonged to Director-General Justice Geoffrey Reed, not Spry.

Another evening, according to Doherty's kids, Mark and Sue-Ellen, they got themselves locked into the subway under the Anzac memorial in Brisbane, behind heavy iron bars. Their father, rather than go through the rigmarole of calling the city council, instead paid the gates a visit with his lock-pick kit and the kids were free immediately. The kit? It was "in a leather roll, like a jewellery roll, only with little pockets. And the triangular tools inside. They got narrower and narrower and narrower. They had points and hooks of all different shapes".

In ASIO's three-volume official history there is no mention of Saffron. The ASIO/Saffron revelations are in a new and extraordinary biography of the Doherty family by journo Sandra Hogan, *With my Little Eye: the incredible true story of a family of spies in the suburbs*.

Dudley and Joan educated their three kids about their ASIO jobs from the time they left their cots. The Dohertys taught them tradecraft against Communists and spies, such as memorising number plates and learning to accurately describe a suspect's clothing, manners and behaviour. They also trained the kids to keep silent on all the secrets of ASIO spying – even from each other, let alone from other family, school — friends and acquaintances. The kids' childhoods were spent in a maze of mirrors where all their bits of ASIO knowledge had to be secretly compartmentalised. For example, the kids must never remark to a Croatian contact about a Serb contact who had dropped in to dinner the night before. Or mention their frequent visitor "Uncle Mick", an ASIO boss.

The Doherty spies used their kids as props. The kids would pose for street photos while Dudley actually focused on suspects behind them. Or Dudley would drive around the block, past Trades Hall or a private house, to monitor suspects. First time, three kids in the front seat. Second pass, two in the back and one hiding on the floor. Further times, they changed clothing and kept popping up and down: "They looked so average they were invisible. They were right there but no one noticed them."

I thought my own childhood was tough growing up as a primary-school Stalinist in a household of Communist Party executives. But my opposite-number kids in their ASIO household had it far tougher.

Brisbane journo Hogan interviewed the Doherty kids as middle-aged adults. At last they could take some family jigsaw pieces out of their brain compartments and fit them together. But none could create a coherent picture of Dad Dudley … and especially not of

PART IV

Dudley's dealings with Saffron.

That connection began during the war, when Dudley graduated from the Salvation Army (playing the euphonium) to the real army at Moorebank depot in southwest Sydney, rising to warrant officer second class. One of his corporals and (literally) procurement specialists was Saffron. But his friendship with Saffron became life-long. Hogan writes,

The wartime period was the only time that Abe worked for Dudley. Later on, the relationship was reversed. Abe served in the army for less than four years before he left to set up Staccato, the first of his strip clubs in Kings Cross, offering a welcome service to the American GIs looking for fun in Sydney.

"He never wasted an opportunity and, while he was in the army, he spotted Dudley's talent for bookkeeping. Abe hired him to do the stocktakes for his clubs, a role Dudley continued to do for the rest of his life, even while he worked for ASIO. Dudley's books were the real ones, which were hidden, while somebody else prepared a different version for the taxation department.

"It would be interesting to know whether Dudley told ASIO about these extra-curricular activities, and how they viewed his work for Abe, but that is one of the many secrets Dudley took to his grave.

It's obvious that Saffron's army "procurements" were lucrative enough to finance his Staccato nightclub.

Mother Joan Doherty was always an upright and loyal citizen.

Hogan writes that she always insisted that, whatever Abe was, Dudley wasn't a criminal—he just liked to stretch things to the limit. 'He was a rogue, but he was a good person,' she said.

Rather improbably, Hogan says Dudley might have swallowed Abe's persona as a family man and a philanthropist and it is possible that Dudley did not know the extent of Abe's crimes. Joan knew from the beginning that Abe was Dudley's friend, but they did not discuss Abe's business life. *By the time Abe had become notorious, Joan would have guessed, perhaps even known, that Abe's hospitality to Dudley included the use of the 'girls' in his brothels; she may have suspected that Dudley knew Abe's books were rigged. But she never believed Dudley knew about the possible murder, drugs and extortion. It probably took a long time for her to believe those things of their old friend, as she was highly sceptical of what she read in the newspapers...*

The bond remained when the Doherty family moved to Brisbane. Joan always put Abe's Christmas cards featuring snow and angels at the front and centre of their collection on the best dresser. Dudley and Joan sometimes holidayed in Sydney at Abe's digs, with treats "on the house" as thank-you's for Dudley's book-keeping.

"Every year, he went down for a few days and helped Abe do his stocktake. It was hard work and he always came back exhausted," the family recalled.

Dudley gave his lad, Mark, at 16 a card for Abe's Pink Pussycat club and told Mark to see Abe in Sydney and get a good time. But Mark "chickened out" of that thorough-going sex education.

PART IV

Joan was a trained observer and no fool, so she must have kept quiet about some of the things she suspected or knew. In an expression from her youth, she 'put up with things'.

> *Secrecy and containment were features of their marriage from beginning to end ... He was away so often from Joan. And there were the prostitutes he visited with oysters, and the girls at Abe's clubs. He said he was working. She kept asking if he was sleeping with other women and he finally admitted it ... He said it was separate, it was work, it didn't have anything to do with them and their undying love. Joan thought about leaving, but what would become of her and the children? She would wait. She was a perfect ASIO wife, supporting Dudley in every way.*

Dudley did, however, get the silent treatment for hours or days. *Joan knew that if she spoke, she might say things that could never be taken back. So she simply took away the warmth of her regard and let him shiver. Despite Dudley's faithlessness, Joan liked to believe that they were equal partners, that she wasn't submissive like her mother, or her sister Clair who was married to a bully.*

The kids realised that Dad might mix with criminals and villains, but that was 'work'. But when Sue-Ellen fell in love with an older man, "suddenly she couldn't help wondering what it actually meant that Abe Saffron was Dad's best friend and that Dad took oysters to visit brothels. Who was her father, really?"

Sue-Ellen eventually met with Dudley's long-time ASIO boss Mick (known to the kids as "Uncle Mick") to seek the truth.

'But how could you be the director and not know what was going on?' she asked him, frustrated. *'That's how we kept secrets,'* he said. *'Well, I think there were things about Dad you didn't know,'* she told him. *'I just don't know if he was everything we thought he was,'* she continued.

'Sue-Ellen, do you think your father was a double agent?' he asked her. *'No. No. But why was he friends with Abe Saffron?'* she blurted out.

'Ah,' he said. *'I can see that would worry you. Well, don't worry too much about it. Your dad served our country well.'* There was something those ASIO men did—she didn't know what it was—but people always ended up telling them everything and they never revealed anything.

The Dohertys were ASIO key workers almost from its inception. Dudley was one of three ASIO eavesdroppers – I won't call them 'buggers' – who bugged a flat above a NSW Communist Party meeting room. Dudley also picked the locks to let them break in.

Joan, too, was an ASIO pioneer, specialising in telephone tapping Soviet MVD/KGB operatives like "Tass correspondent" Fedor Nosov. She worked 'behind a green door' in a basement in ASIO headquarters typing up recordings made on a Pyrox wire recorder. She kept this work secret even from her fellow spy and husband Dudley, little knowing that Dudley himself had helped install the taps.

Joan left ASIO when her first child was born, but the Dohertys continued living in a flat alongside Nosov in Darlinghurst, assisting the phone taps. It must have been a crowded flat with ASIO officers also there working in shifts round the clock monitoring the devices.

"She recalled that she tiptoed around the flat and her children wore slippers so that the ASIO officers could listen to what was happening without hearing thudding in their headphones. She made coffee and fed the officers on duty," Horner writes.

Later the Dohertys ran a house for the Petrovs in Northcliffe, Qld. The Petrovs were not trouble-free boarders. One night Vladimir was arrested while drunk after he tried to enter a residence at Surfers Paradise that he mistook for his flat. He got into a fight with the residents, which destroyed his trousers. (Malcolm Fraser would sympathise.) Police took him to the Southport Police Station, charged him with drunkenness and released him the next morning on ten shillings' bail (forfeited, says Horner).

I happened to read Sandra Hogan's book With *My Little Eye* and its ASIO/Saffron revelations mere days before watching the ABC's Caro Meldrum-Hanna's expose on police and other corruption concerning the Ghost Train arson and Abe Saffron. What value was ASIO boss Spry getting from Saffron? I asked myself, What was ASIO's relationship with Saffron from 1970 (Doherty's death) to 1979 (the Ghost Train fire) and thereafter? It's obvious that ASIO senior spy Doherty was personally corrupt. How corrupt was ASIO? #

The Hilaria-ous Case of the Pseudo Señora

1 January 2021

Escandalo! Among Hollywood's Trump-hating and climate-doom celebrities, actor Alec Baldwin stands tall. I've enjoyed his *Glengarry Glen Ross* movie several times, but he's a nasty person with sadistic impulses. Plus he's another of those Hollywood hypocrites, splashing his $US60 million wealth on big houses and big toys in New York, while telling the plebs to catch buses and eat lentils. He sees both "climate denial" and voting for Donald Trump as forms of mental illness.

His wife, Hillary runs a yoga business. She calls herself Hilaria, born in Majorca, but turns out to be Boston-born Hillary Hayward-Thomas (no relation to me). She brought mirth down upon Alec this week. A decade ago she adopted a Spanish persona and accent, plus a Spanish life history rich in paella and flamenco dancing. On a TV cooking show, the Latino lady even had trouble with that English tongue-twister 'cucumber' : "We have tomatoes, we have, um, how you say in Eng — cucumbers."

The narrative fell apart after Hillary/Hilaria posted an inspirational pic of herself in saucy black lingerie and holding Eduardo, her latest of five Baldwinito babies. Comic Amy Schumer re-posted the pic on her own Christmas card with a message: "Enjoy it with whatever family members are talking to you this year." Hillary/Hilaria, who it seems isn't very bright, didn't get the joke and accused Schumer of "body-shaming" her as a recent mother who

PART IV

happened to have shed all trace of flab. While they were duking it out on Instagram, a Hillary ex-classmate who goes by the pseudonym of "Leni Briscoe" (a name that might or might not have been inspired by Law & Order detective Lenny Briscoe), tweeted: 'You have to admire Hilaria Baldwin's commitment to her decade-long grift where she impersonates a Spanish person.'

Hillary didn't re-invent herself for money: she's worth $US10 million thanks to book and TV deals gathered on her husband's coat-tails. She's also an unofficial brand ambassador for Tommee Tippee baby bottles. She grew up in a five-bedroom Boston mansion in swanky Beacon Hill, almost next door to ex-Secretary of State John Kerry. Now she's under fire for hogging space in Latin magazines and shows and appropriating the identity of a woke-designated victim class. In 2016, for example, she posted indignantly about how often she is stopped and asked if she's a nanny because she speaks Spanish.

The angsts of minor celebs is normally beneath the notice of Quadrant writers and readers. But Hillary's husband's contortions over the affair, coupled with his extensive record of general nastiness and hypocrisy, are too fruity for a local hack like myself to ignore. Alec fulminated in support of his wife , "It is troubling to watch people lie about what you have said and not said. You are the most principled and decent woman I have ever known."

It was barely a week ago that Alec Baldwin was tweeting to the million followers of his Hilaria and Alec Baldwin Foundation account that if Trump refuses to concede, he should be violently killed, a la George Floyd in Minneapolis. "The thug who has destroyed the country. What does he deserve?" Baldwin asked. "A knee on his neck, cutting off his oxygen? Does he wheeze 'I can't breathe?'" He also proposed that Trump be beaten in the way four policemen beat Rodney King in Los Angeles in 1991, which led to arson and riots. "Just whale away on him like a piñata? Rodney King style?" Baldwin suggested.

Last month Baldwin called for President Trump to be buried in a Nazi graveyard with a swastika placed on his grave. One responder added, "No. he does not deserve a burial. Dump him in an unmarked grave or better yet in a crematorium." Baldwin has also called Trump a "fascist whore" needing to be "removed from our lives". The multi-racial supporters whom Trump enlisted at his National Convention in August were, according to Baldwin, high on drugs.

In February, Baldwin likened Trump's rise to power to that of Adolf Hitler, saying, "You wonder how Hitler took control of a once great country. For those of you too young to remember the War or its aftermath, simply watch how this [Republican] Senate behaves. Their snivelling fealty and lack of courage… And you begin to get it."

In May, Baldwin declared that President Trump "has a degenerative mental illness that is costing 1000's of lives." He tweeted, a little histrionically, "Trump's presidency must die so that we can live."

PART IV

As for every movie star's hobby of saving the planet, Baldwin said at the Paris 2015 summit that "this may be our last chance in the next 20 years" to take action against global warming. "There are things that we just can't imagine that can happen in terms of the food supply, in terms of climate change, in terms of flooding in coastal areas in the United States and beyond," he said. "The time is now to make certain sacrifices ... so that this planet will remain habitable for today's children."

Alec Baldwin's bad temper is documented from way back. In a custody dispute over his daughter, Ireland, with mother Kim Basinger in 2007, Basinger's lawyers surfaced a voicemail of him abusing the daughter as a 'rude, thoughtless, little pig'. He told her, "You don't have the brains or the decency as a human being. ... I don't give a damn that you're 12 years old, or 11 years old, or that you're a child, or that your mother is a thoughtless pain in the ass who doesn't care about what you do as far as I'm concerned ... You have humiliated me for the last time with this phone."

Getting back to his spouse's Dunciad, Hillary once told Vanity Fair España that her "Spanish" parents had difficulty pronouncing her married surname "Baldwin". Actually, Mama is Harvard med-school ex-professor, Dr. Kathryn Hayward, whose family is fourth-generation Boston Brahmin, and Pop is David Thomas, a Georgetown educated lawyer hailing from Vermont. (As already mentioned, not a relative of mine).

Now Hillary has admitted she's Boston born, saying: "Yes, I am a white girl Let's be very clear that Europe has a lot of white people in there and my family is white. Ethnically, I am a mix of many, many, many things. Culturally, I grew up with two cultures so it's really as simple as that." She further explains, "I care because my thing is about being authentic — and then if people say I'm not being authentic, it hurts my feelings … " She asked social media gawkers at her part-clad pics to be "a little bit kinder," especially after a year when everybody is "suffering mentally."

Perhaps her least likely claims were that she'd never owned a TV set and that when she fell for the ageing Alec, she had no idea that he was a movie star. "So what do you do?" she supposedly asked him, guilelessly. He's 62, she's 36, by the way.

Somehow borrowing identities is quite a trend. Apart from Democrat icon Elizabeth "Pocahontas" Warren, there is the famous Rachel Dolezal, aka Nkechi Amare Diallo, who despite her two white parents rose as a "black" woman to chapter presidency of the National Association for the Advancement of Colored People.

The pinnacle of role-snaffling was reached by left-feminist author/academic Jessica Krug, who claimed variously to be half-Algerian-American, half-German-American, and an "Afro-boricua" from The Bronx, nicknamed "La Bombalera." She admitted in September she was actually a Jewish lass from Kansas, who had lied first about North African blackness, then US-rooted blackness, then Caribbean-rooted Bronx blackness.

Not that we are immune from such things in Australia. Between the 2011 and 2016 censuses, 130,000 people newly-identified as Aboriginal. Many claimants had compelling reasons but at least one New Age lady learnt she was Aboriginal via conversations with her chooks, and featured in one of those erudite Griffith MA theses. A recent spectacular Aboriginal identification was by "Aboriginal historian" Bruce Pascoe, now a Professor at an obscure Melbourne university, whose four grandparents are from the UK, and who mysteriously claims to be both "solidly Cornish" and "solidly Aboriginal".

As for Mr and Mrs Baldwin, there's a moral from their discomfiture, which in my native tongue of Spanish is: *Me importa un pepino.* (I don't give a cucumber). #

The Academic Murderer: Maurice Benn's Family Tragedy

29 March 2020

For reasons that now escape me, I started my part-time studies at WA University in 1959 with two years of German language and literature. My lecturer and guide was Dr Maurice Benn, the newly-installed head of German. A few years later Mr Justice Hale in the WA Supreme Court put on his black cap with one corner facing forward (actually it's just a piece of black cloth, of Tudor origin), and sentenced Dr Benn to hang by the neck until he was dead for wilful murder. I'm writing about Dr Benn to clear some more debris from my cranial attic.

Benn seemed born to dwell in cloisters writing tracts for other lovers of classic German literature. We junior students instead snickered at his too-short trouser legs showing colourful socks. He would declaim German poets with deep feeling, like Rilke's "Carousel" (Das Karussell) with its catch-line, 'Und dann und wann ein weisser Elefant" referring to the merry-go-round journey of the white elephant. Why do the few things I recall from uni days include that line recited by Dr Benn?

He was kindly and tolerant of stupid freshers. We gathered at lunchtimes to sing German folk (Die Lorelei) and student songs (Annie of Tharau), which continue as ear-worms in my head. I liked proximity to girls, then an alien species, and I managed to date a co-chorister harmlessly for a month or so.

For this article's sake, I phoned her from Melbourne after a

PART IV

gap of 60 years to see what she remembered of Dr Benn and surreptitiously, of myself. This is a common fantasy among codgers, but rarely implemented. I connected after dialling only two numbers. She remembered zilch of Dr Benn and zilch of myself.

Dr Benn marked my essays with more care than I ever spent writing them. I struggled with Goethe's novel "Sorrows of Young Werther", despite Dr Benn's help. Young Werther shot himself over love for Charlotte, married to another. It was the late 18th-century's *Fifty Shades of Grey*. All over Europe young men dressed like Werther and suffered what they called "Werther fever". In England Thackeray got the continental ambience right:

> *WERTHER had a love for Charlotte*
>
> *Such as words could never utter;*
>
> *Would you know how first he met her?*
>
> *She was cutting bread and butter ...*
>
> *Charlotte, having seen his body*
>
> *Borne before her on a shutter,*
>
> *Like a well-conducted person,*
>
> *Went on cutting bread and butter.*

We students had scant curiosity about our lecturers but I've now found some fragments about Benn. He was born in Glasgow in

1914 and the family came to Perth in 1928. Benn played piano ("wonderfully", one of Benn's friends tells me) and viola chamber music with his brothers George (violin and viola) and Tom (cello). George suicided in 1939 and Tom joined the blue-collar ranks of the Communist Party.

In 1939 Maurice Benn was on his way to London on a Hackett Studentship. The war broke out and he returned to Perth (one version is that his ship turned back before reaching London).

He enlisted in the navy in 1941 -- he wasn't as prissy as we thought. He finished his London and Zurich studies post-war, returning to UWA in 1952 with nervous German bride Irena – he'd married her a year earlier. She was one of his pupils during his English classes at a school near Zurich. He was 38, she 24.

Benn's eventual home was in Portland Street, Nedlands, a kilometre from the campus. He would run evenings for students and staff for music and discussion. He helped set up the local Goethe Society (student annual dues: 35 cents) and filled Winthrop Hall with 600 people for the bi-centenary Goethe concert in 1949. Try replicating that today!

The Benns longed for a child. After eight years Irena had a son Bernard Wolfgang, the same year I enrolled with Maurice.

Sadly, the boy's brain was awry. He was described in court as a small wild animal, uncontrollable and not even recognising his parents. He seemed destined for an institution, and for adult life at Perth's archaic Claremont Asylum: in language of the day, "The

PART IV

Looney-Bin". For Irena, dealing with his fits and ferocity was a nightmare.

The crisis came on February 8, 1964. Benn 49, told the jury of eight men and four women that he got an irresistible idea of killing Bernard, who was four and a half but assessed at one-year-old mentally.

Benn feared Irena would break down or take her own life. He wrote her, "My dear Irena, I didn't dare tell you before ... But the Doctor told me Bernard would never lead a normal, happy life ... he will have to go through his whole life in a state of mental derangement ... I must save him from such a terrible fate at all costs ... and you from complete collapse." He signed it "With love" and left it on his study table.

Then he took a .22 rifle he had always kept in the study (I still find that rifle incongruous). The boy was asleep in his cot. Benn testified, "I thought it would save the boy from a terrible kind of life, that I would save my wife. It seemed I just had to do it. I remember pointing the rifle at the boy's temple. I remember the shot and I saw blood coming from the boy's temple." Then he rang the police to turn himself in.

Irena 36, testified she was having a shower that night and heard a very strange noise. She called but Maurice didn't reply. She put on her husband's dressing gown and again cried very loudly, "Maurice".

He stood between the bathroom and the boy's room and had a

very strange expression on his face—as if he was mad."

"And then he said, 'I have shot Bernard.' I don't remember what happened then. I screamed all the time."

The court reporters found Benn calm and sincere. He believed he'd done the right thing but accepted that he'd be punished.

Benn's barrister was K.T. Hatfield and solicitor was John Wheeldon, later the most Communist-minded of all in Prime Minister Whitlam's ministry. They pleaded temporary overwhelming insanity for Benn, but the judge was having none of it. Killing was killing and Benn knew what he was doing. He told the jury to take all emotion out of the equation.

The jury misunderstood further instructions to mean that any recommendation for mercy had to be unanimous, so they brought in 'guilty' with no rider for mercy. Hence came the sentence of death by hanging. Irena collapsed. Later she told the press, "Maurice is no criminal; he did it because he loved both of us."

For a fortnight the noose dangled over Dr Benn, then Premier Dave Brand's L-CP government commuted death to ten years' hard labour, or about seven before parole. Benn didn't actually break rocks; "hard labour" began with clerical work in the Fremantle store. His cell included a bookshelf, table, chair and a higher-wattage lamp for studying from 5pm to 'lights out' at 8. He was also allowed to have books in foreign languages.

At the time parents of unfortunate children got little aid. Some still isolated their offspring at home to protect them from other kids' taunts. Letters to papers nationally in the wake of the Benn conviction included a number from parents saying they had contemplated killing their child. Some hinted that parents had killed such children in staged accidents. As one woman put it, "Every one of us would have been relieved to see our child die. Perhaps the only reason that our husbands have not stood trial for murder is due to one of two things -- the good fortune to have had a sound spiritual background, or the lack of courage to commit euthanasia for fear of the consequences."

The male secretary of a Slow Learning Children's branch wrote that "Mongol" children should be compulsorily admitted to State care: "I know the heartbreak of losing one's children would be of comparatively short duration – time heals all things. Release these unfortunate parents from their burden by law, and we should never have a crime like the Benn case on our conscience again." He was immediately sacked.

There was even a letter seeking legal changes to permit some infant children "to be put to rest" via court orders. But others countered that mercy killings of the unfortunate would be no better than Hitler's culling of the unfit.

Perth's high-brow community assumed cabinet would set Benn free after minor prison time, but their megaphone diplomacy only fed the Brand ministry's anti-intellectual paranoia.

Academia rallied to Benn's support, led by UWA Chancellor Sir

Alex Reid. UWA quickly found Irena a job tutoring in German, which brings myself back into the story a bit.

The West Australian, where I ranked as a D or C Grade Reporter, suspected the job was a sinecure for the murderer's wife and since I had the title Education Writer, I was briefed to track her down for a 'gotcha' interview.

The chief of staff tightened the screws on me for an Irena Benn scoop because of an incident way out of left field. Father E. J. Stormon was Rector of the gracious Thomas More Residential College by the university and overlooking Matilda Bay. On March 23, a fortnight before Benn's verdict, an 18yo newbie called David refused the traditional initiation. A dozen lads from good Catholic families bounced him in his room two nights later and painted his face with silver nitrate, causing second-degree burns later needing hospital treatment. They bound him hand and foot and drove him 25km east to the industrial wilds of Kenwick. There they stripped him, painted his genitals with black shoe-polish and left him in his underpants (or singlet, take your choice) in a shallow creek, to struggle back to Crawley.

David's mother blew the whistle on the college, but cruelly blew it to our afternoon sibling *Daily News* rather than myself. Father Stormon explained that it was just a prank that got out of hand: no brutality intended but some irresponsibility shown. The perpetrators "were of good character and respected by other students and staff". They were sorry about it and Stormon hoped the incident was now closed, after he fined the boys an undisclosed amount.

PART IV

So I'd go to the Arts Faculty which I knew well as a part-timer, to flush out Mrs Benn. The staff would spot me, alert Irena, and she'd go to ground. Pursuing Irena was bad for my soul; I had pleasant memories of her husband. Eventually I lived down being scooped on boot-blacked genitals and my chief of staff found other fish to fry than Irena Benn, who went on to teach German to a generation of girls at one of Perth's private schools, either MLC or PLC.

For nearly five long years Irena visited Maurice each second Sunday, mostly at his low-security rehab centre at Karnet, 70km south of Perth. His job there was librarian. He was failing in health not just physically but mentally from lack of intellectual company. His book manuscript on the 19th Century poet Hoelderlin was accepted by Oxford University Press, London, shades of Mel Gibson's movie "The Professor and the Madman".

UWA librarian Leonard Jolley, a fellow-lover of German classics and possessor of a whiplash tongue, joined Sir Alex in the fight to free Benn and also provided Benn with a vital flow of arcane literary texts and critiques.

Author Mary Durack led WA writers in support of freedom for Benn. Her daughter Patsy Millett says, "There was a bit more to the story [of Maurice's crisis] than is on record, involving Irena's constant and frantic calls to him while he was lecturing at UWA. She would be telling him he must come home to deal with Bernard. He simply could not take it any longer."

Unusually, the State's top gaoler Colin Campbell, Comptroller-General of Prisons, strongly urged Benn's early release. Another advocate for Benn was his Probation and Parole officer Dr Bill Matsdorf, historian of the Kimberley Jewish homeland project. Matsdorf was so disgusted with Benn's treatment that he moved permanently to Israel.

In early 1968 the Parole Board recommended Benn be freed, but cabinet stubbornly announced a deferral for 12 months. He was released on parole in December from Karnet, where he'd become more guest than prisoner. All-up he served four and a half years. He and Irena were provided with a secret home-stay in the hills and Benn became a UWA Senior Research Fellow on salary of $9,900 (today's money: $120,000). In March 1969 they left for a sabbatical in Europe, unbeknownst to the press. He died of a heart attack in 1975. In 2011 a large gift of German books went to the UWA library from the collection of Maurice and Irena Benn.

Irena's friend Patsy Millett says Irena later moved to Tyrell St, Nedlands and other than for a few friends (including the wife of a former WA governor and Perth author/academic Sister Veronica Brady, of Loreto) she led a pretty lonely – very Catholic - life.

Patsy says, "After most of her friends and supporters died in the 1990s, I became her closest carer and kept her going at home as she descended into senility. We had many an outing to symphony concerts, Perth Festival films and to the river, where I got her into the water to bathe. She liked a laugh.

"Then home care became no longer possible. I still live with the awful memory of the day I delivered her to the Mercy Care home in Wembley. She died in 2013 and her estate passed to a never-met niece and nephew in Germany (not so much as a card of thanks from them to those who had devotedly looked after their aunt)."

My personal story has one last sequel. My cousin Phil Allen was head English teacher at Perth's selective Modern School. I visited for my class's 50-year reunion in October 2007, and Phil invited me to address a class of his high-achievers about journalism. I thought he wanted a talk on clear writing/journalese and prepared accordingly. On the spot however he told the kids that I'd wow them about my colourful career.

I'm not a good ad-libber for 35 minutes and after some pleasantries about the art of shorthand, I described how in 1957 we'd found a girl's knickers in the gym and run it (or them?) up the school flagpole. I hadn't realised how *verboten* such tales are among modern high schoolers.

Then I stumbled my way into the Dr Benn story. Searching for words to describe the son Bernard's wildness and the fatal torment imposed on the father, I mis-described the murdered child in slang as "hopeless".

It turned out that one lad in the class had a kid brother who was seriously autistic. The lad was anxious about the impacts of his brother on his mother's mental health, and I'd just recounted how a parent had chosen to kill. The lad told all to his mother that night, and she was rightly appalled. She got on the phone to Phil and gave him a blast.

Phil did some fancy moves to extricate himself from the Benn-story tentacles I had wrapped him in. Moreover he hadn't even sought approval for my class visit. But his career survived. We also survived the knickers story, one of Phil's 13yo students merely describing me on her feedback paper as 'immature'. Phil and I remain pals, but he never invited me back to his class.

It feels good now to have unloaded all this Benn material. Next time we complain that it's tough with COVID-19, recall Maurice and Irena Benn and their son Bernard. #

PART IV

Memories of the Really Wild West

13 March 2020

The Perth of my youth was a friendly town, half asleep by the bays and reaches of the Swan. We called ourselves the "Wildflower State". Perhaps the "Flogging and Hanging State" would be more apt. First, I'll reminisce about the hangings, then the floggings.

In 1964 when I was a reporter and part-time UWA student, there were three death sentences, and two were carried out. Perth's Anglican Archbishop, the Most Rev George Appleton, protested but added that if the death penalty had to stay, the State should switch to lethal injections. To be fair to my home state, the October 1964 hanging of random sniper Eric Edgar Cooke was WA's last; Victoria's Liberal premier, Henry Bolte, hanged escapee/murderer Robert Ryan three years later, the last man to go to the gallows in Australia.

Perth authorities hanged Brian William Robinson in January 1964, the same year that saw Cooke hanged. The Robinson preliminaries were so off-the-wall that I don't expect to be believed. Perth wasn't *like* the Wild West, it *was* the Wild West. Thousands of viewers of Channel 7 Perth armed themselves to help the police capture the desperado in a pine plantation, at extreme risk of death by friendly fire. The policing culture has become gentler since those rough-hewn days, e.g., Victoria Police's sensitivities about shooting crazed Dimitrious Gargasoulas before his death-dealing car rampage down Bourke Street Mall in 2017.

On Saturday morning, 9 February 1963, Robinson, 23, ran amok after hearing a rumour that his mother was also his sister. (A milder version maintains that the catalyst was father George, 70, chipping him for dole-bludging). Constable Noel Iles was called to the fracas at the family's Belmont home as the Robinsons were fighting for a shotgun. Getting control of the weapon, son Brian Robinson turned it on Iles and from a front window shot him in the face. Then he went outside, kicked the kneeling Iles over and shot him in the head, fatally. A pair in a passing Goggomobile Dart convertible (a 300cc microcar) stopped to look. Robinson tried for a Goggomobile getaway and shot the passenger dead when he resisted. The woman driver stayed in the car and was filmed by Channel 7's crew, hot on the scene, smoking a cigarette in a holder with the body in a blanket slumped behind her.

Robinson then commandeered a Swan taxi by whacking the driver Arthur Smith with the gun-butt. The army-trained driver got out a may-day call. He drove Robinson to the Gnangara pine plantation and deliberately bogged the taxi a couple of kilometres inside. They made off on foot and the Smith got away when Robinson hid from a police spotter plane.

When night fell the police manhunters relied on an RAAF searchlight truck and Channel 7's Outside Broadcast Van's studio lights and microwave communications. In this fraternal atmosphere police asked young Seven reporter Bob Cribb to broadcast a call for all available personnel to come to the plantation, armed. The police meant "off-duty police" but newsreader Lloyd Lawson called on armed citizens of every description. Incredibly, the police directed Cribb to enter the plantation with the Seven van only if he had a gun. He borrowed a shotgun from his local greengrocer, additional to pen, pad and mike.

Sniper Eric Edgar Cooke, "The Night Caller", was at large after shooting five residents in the previous five weeks. Multitudes of Perth men had weapons handy to defend hearth and home. Posses arrived at the plantation in their thousands, by car, truck, motorbike, bicycle and horseback, armed with shotguns, rifles and pistols. The estimate was a 5000-strong force, police included and a few Amazonian women. Many police were out of uniform and none of the crowd knew what Robinson looked like. TV footage shows one street crammed end-to-end for a kilometre with armed Perth-ites. Some were in cowboy hats with rifle in one hand and pistol in the other.

Policeman Bob Masters was on the front line: "I was just astounded when I came on the back of Robbie Drew's motorbike [was that Robert Drew the future novelist?]. We went the full length of the road, people were right alongside each other, they had guns, it really worried me, it was terrible." Nonetheless the police were not averse to helpers. One high-ranking officer addressed the crowd about the danger, "and if we felt uncomfortable, we were given permission to leave," says reporter Colin Gorey.

The makeshift army "proceeded with daring abandon through deep undergrowth," the Seven newsreader intoned. Long lines of manhunters strode forward, filmed by Channel 7's crew in the spirit of Damien Parer on the Kokoda Track. Live outside TV in 1963 was in its infancy, so the black and white action footage was stunning. Reporter Cribb ad-libbed for three hours, including such sub-judice gems as "The mad dog killer is holed up in this bush".

The most solid account is by retired WA Police Commissioner Brian Bull, who as a young detective helped organise the manhunt. He recounts that as they approached the abandoned taxi a shot rang out – but from a fumbling policeman. During the night the perimeter was cordoned and by daylight police brought in a "native tracker" Mick Wilson, who had been holidaying from Port Hedland. Bull's job was to closely protect the tracker from the gunman, with six police 200m in reserve behind: "I admired the courage of Mick who was completely exposed if we came close to the offender and he was the one most likely to be fired upon." I find no report that Mick got an award. After many hours Mick said the killer was near. Everyone closed up and then several shots rang out. But they were from the blocking line of police ahead, and they brought down the fleeing Robinson.

In his understated police way, Bull said his group hadn't realised they were walking into the path of the massed public and police gunnies. "It became evident that we had been exposed to considerable risk from 'friendly fire' and it was fortunate that the offender was shot before many police and armed members of the public opened fire," he concluded. Policeman Bob Masters fired that final shot: "If I hadn't, I believe a lot of other people would

PART IV

have been badly injured."

Robinson was convicted in May 1963 and hanged on January 20, 1964.

Reporter Cribb, a colourful and likeable guy, was later fired by Seven three or four times and re-instated, doubtless thanks to the channel's scoop of the century. Cameraman Peter Goodall wrote: "It was crazy. We all got back to Seven and were elated. Even invited to the board room for champagne. Some crazy memories … mmm!"

This might all whet your appetite for Fremantle's history of floggings, the western city today being one of the country's most woke.

Flogging was on the WA statutes until 1992, but the last thrashing involved a 19-year-old shop assistant in 1962. He got two years and 12 strokes of the birch for consensual sex with a 14-year-old, a.k.a. "unlawful carnal knowledge". He appealed the sentence but the aptly named Chief Justice Mr Justice Wolff said it was "richly deserved". A QC, Tom Percy, commented, "He wasn't old enough to vote, or even have a drink, but in the eyes of the law he was old enough to be flogged." Who did the flogging and how it was carried out remains a state secret, although we do know the Brand Liberal government imported the birch rod specially from England. The previous birching was said to have been in the late 1950s.

The last full-on flogging with a cat-o-nine tails in Fremantle Gaol involved robber Sydney Sutton 43, for escaping gaol (he made a key in the workshop) and raping a 12-year-old schoolgirl. That flogging took place on June 22, 1943, not 1843. He'd also committed rape during an escape from the lower-security Barton's Mill.

Sutton was inside Fremantle since 1937 for housebreaking, robbery with violence and for a movie-style shoot-out with detectives on Canning Bridge. His terms totalled 81 years. Not lacking initiative, he briefly enjoyed three weeks' freedom in 1939-40 as well, by escaping in a brown felt hat from a working party that was burning off grass outside. Gaol was "a hell of a life", he complained to the beak, Mr H.J. Craig.

For the 1943 escape and rape, Sutton was sentenced to life and 25 lashes of the cat. Fear immediately sent him into a medical collapse. Perth lacked a hangman/flogger but scores of Perth and Eastern States police, warders and amateurs clamoured for the job. Newspapers printed letters from volunteers pressing their case.

Sutton was tied to the triangle with hands above his head and ankles secured. The Mirror reported,

> *Though he has shown contempt for every other form of punishment, a flogging was more than even a hardened criminal of Sutton's type could stand. And by the time the cat had bitten into his back 17 times, a doctor examined the writhing, moaning man and decided that was all he could bear for the present. His back, streaked with the marks of the lashes, was carefully tended by the doctor and Sutton was taken away.* [I hope the doctor bulk-billed].

PART IV

> *As news of the flogging seeped through the prison, the effect on the other prisoners was profound. Of all jail punishments, none has a greater effect on a man's fellow prisoners – and presumably his former associates outside – than a flogging. It is intended as a deterrent, grisly and fear-impelling, but not sadistic.*

After a public outcry, Sutton was let off the remaining eight lashes. In fact, undeterred by that 'non-sadistic' experience, he was caught hiding in the prison roof space on July 22, exactly a month later.

Perth people in the 1960s had few degrees of separation, and even now you need to watch what you say and to whom. As a reporter, I knew Labor Deputy Opposition Leader Herb Graham a bit. He was not only an anti-hanging and anti-flogging crusader in the Assembly, but had actually seen Sutton in gaol a few months after the flogging. (Graham was truly a political veteran, having entered State Parliament in early 1943). After seeing Sutton, Graham brought a cat o' nine tails into the Assembly "for the edification of members", much like Prime Minister Morrison arriving in the House in 2016 with a lump of coal.

In a 1965 Assembly debate, Graham said, "That person [Sutton] had the look of a mad animal. I could almost see him snarl as we approached him. I suggest that was brought about by what he had to suffer in the way of the lashing."

Flogging was not an abstruse issue in 1965. Perth gays, for example, were liable not merely to a maximum 14 years hard labour for buggery, but a whipping. "Gross indecency" involved only three years, but also with a whipping. Buggery convictions occurred from time to time — a former high-school classmate of mine was charged after a gay fancy-dress party where revellers dressed like nuns. Sentences were fairly token but the public disgrace was severe.

Deputy Premier Charlie Court brought in a Bill to tone down the words using in sentencing murderers. Judges heretofore used to say that the "prisoner be returned to his former custody, and that at a time and place to be appointed by the Governor, he be hanged by the neck until he is dead."

But thanks to Liberal compassion, the wording was to be changed to "suffer death in the manner prescribed by law". No change ensued to isolation, hangman imported from interstate, a padre's supplications, calculation of drops, noose, and greased trapdoor hinge. The 1965 Bill also varied the whippings procedure, to substitute a cane or leather strap for the hard-to-procure birch rods.

Charlie Court didn't take Graham seriously, saying the Bill was just legislative tidying-up:

> *Court: We have heard the member with this standard speech of his so often.*
>
> *Graham: No, it is different every time I make it.*

Court chided that in the election earlier that year, hardly a constituent had raised the issue of hanging. Moreover, parents of young girls were keen on rapists getting whipped.

Court continued, "It is easy to get emotionally worked up over these matters but the Government feels they have to be considered and decided in a calmer atmosphere. The Government is keeping this matter constantly under review in a sensible and responsible way." In the event, WA's capital punishment law lingered for 19 years, including the eight years of Court's premiership, until Labor's WA Inc. Premier Brian Burke grasped the nettle in 1984. Corporal punishment stayed on the books till 1992.

Personally I remember getting flogged by my mother about 1948 for stealing 10 shillings from her purse to spend on fireworks – quite a sum in those days. She used a bunch of leather straps on my calves, not realising that a single strap would be more painful. It hardly hurt but I yelled anyway. #

The Madman of Tullamarine

31 October 2012

There is much to be said about the joys of children, but words are apt to fail any parent marooned without a car key in an airport's tow-away zone. Well, not all words ...

I was required to deliver one of my daughters, Briony, to Melbourne's Tullamarine Airport the other day. She drove her car with me in the passenger seat.

On arrival at Tullamarine, the 3-minute parking bays for departures were pretty full. I pointed to a small gap and said, "Stick your bonnet in there, it doesn't matter if the car's backside is sticking out because I'll be on my way home with the car in no time."

I got out and gallantly went round to the boot to unload her uber-heavy cases. With an affectionate farewell, daughter disappeared into the terminal, bound for Singapore.

I paused to give the sigh of fatherhood, then went round to the driver's seat and leaned forward to key-start the car. But the key was not there. Daughter had taken it with her into the terminal.

I felt like a lab rat in an experiment designed to induce mental collapse. I could stay in car and hope daughter would re-emerge from the terminal. That would mean overstaying the 3 minutes and moreover, every minute I sat there increased the chance that daughter would go into the one-way immigration hall.

PART IV

I could instead abandon the car and dash into the terminal in the hope of discovering daughter and wrenching the keys violently from her. This would mean the security guards would notice an abandoned car parked at 45 degrees to the footpath and with its backside sticking out a metre or two (all the other cars had meanwhile driven away leaving daughter's car alone and prominent). At best, car would be towed away; at worst, blown up.

I chose to abandon the car and try to locate my daughter, and dashed into International Terminal. Milling crowds everywhere, and I had no idea which airline Briony was using. So I took up a position five metres inside, and shouted at the top of my lungs: "B-R-I-O-N-Y !!" This caused a sensation as people wondered who the elderly male was and why he was screaming. Briony failed to appear.

I checked the departures: a QANTAS 380 was boarding for Singapore. I dashed to the right to the special QANTAS section where hundreds of travellers were coiling around the people-barriers like a snakes and ladders game. Briony is short and if there, she would be undetectable. So I again bellowed, 'B-R-I-O-N-Y !!" Again the crowd gave a startle-response but no Briony emerged. Staff are still talking about "the Madman of Tullamarine" they saw that day.

By this time I was fearful about my daughter's abandoned car. I dashed outside and sat in it, not realising that I could at least release the handbrake and push the car to align it with the kerb. But Briony by now could possibly be ticketed and heading for

Immigration. I needed to go back again to seek her out among the multitude.

I dashed back into the terminal, dashed here, dashed there, and then looked back and caught sight of a group of officers outside the terminal, some armed, warily inspecting my daughter's grey runabout. I dashed outside again to liaise with the security squad. "This is your car?" they asked, grim-faced.

Myself, doing a little dance of anxiety: "Yes, that's right, no, daughter's! She's in there somewhere [gesticulating towards terminal]. Suitcases…she drove… Singapore… no key … a good girl, usually … sure to come out soon with key … on my mother's grave, I'm not al Qaeda! Can one of you please hotwire this car? Please don't tow an old pensioner away!" [Actually I have a Senior's Card but am not a pensioner].

None of my pleas impressed the bomb squad. They circled round the car like it was a wild beast, or a big pile of steaming ordure. Some wrote copiously in black-covered notebooks, others dialled up colleagues or maybe the SOGGIES [Special Operations Group] on their radio. They were joined by a parking inspector demanding me to justify why my car was so badly parked. While I was again explaining, a familiar figure holding car keys burst out of the terminal, my daughter Briony!

She explained everything to the blue-clad commandos. She had been excited about her big trip to Singapore. She got her tickets. She remembered she had a letter to post and went to the airport

PART IV

Post Office. She pulled the letter out of her handbag and noticed the car keys. She put two and two together and thought I might need them. That's all, officers, it's quite a simple mistake.

The security squad conferred and wandered off, disappointed. The parking lady continued tapping busily into her fines device, ignoring my daughter's increasingly shrill protests. Parking lady: "I'm just doing my job. Have a nice day". And to me, "On your way, please."

"Heck Dad! It's your fault. You should pay the fines. Why didn't you ask me for the keys!"

With another fatherly sigh, the Madman of Tullamarine headed for home in Briony's grey Nissan Tiida.

#